S0-FQX-324

English as a Second Language

Helen Brennan Memorial Library

Milestones

An Intermediate Reader/Workbook in English

Robert L. Saitz
Boston University

John M. Kopec
Boston University

English as a Second Language

Helen Brennan Memorial Library

Little, Brown and Company
Boston • Toronto

Copyright © 1987 by Robert L. Saitz and John M. Kopec

Library of Congress Cataloging-in-Publication Data

Saitz, Robert L.
   Milestones : an intermediate reader/workbook in
English.

   1. English language — Text-books for foreign speakers.
2. Readers — 1950–   I. Kopec, John M. II. Title.
PE1128.S2168 1986   428.6′4   86-20013
ISBN 0-316-76703-4

All rights reserved. No part of this book may be reproduced in any form or by any electronic or mechanical means including information storage and retrieval systems without permission in writing from the publisher, except by a reviewer who may quote brief passages in a review.

Library of Congress Catalog Card No. 86-20013

ISBN 0-316-76703-4

9 8 7 6 5 4 3 2 1

Illustrations on pages 2, 24, 56, 84, 124, 137, 156, 184, 220, 238, and 240 by Luis Miguel Muelle, copyright © 1987 by Little, Brown and Company, Inc.

Published simultaneously in Canada
by Little, Brown & Company (Canada) Limited

Printed in the United States of America

MV

Credits

   Gordon Lish, "Fear." From "Fear: Four Examples" in *What I Know So Far* by Gordon Lish. Copyright © 1977, 1978, 1979, 1980, 1981, 1983, 1984. Reprinted by permission of Henry Holt & Company. **Wilt Chamberlain,** "My First Car." From an interview by Marian Long with Wilt Chamberlain, *Gentlemen's Quarterly,* July 1984. Courtesy *Gentlemen's Quarterly.* Copyright © 1984 by The Condé Nast Publications Inc. **Bob Greene,** "A Thanksgiving Memory." From Bob Greene, *Johnny Deadline, Reporter* (Chicago, 1976), pp. 54–56, by permission of Nelson-Hall, Publishers. **Maia Wojciechowska,** "The First Day of the War." From *Till the Break of Day* by Maia Wojciechowska. Copyright © 1972 by Maia Wojciechowska. All rights reserved. Reprinted by permission of the Author's Representative, Gunther Stuhlmann. **Samuel F. O'Gorman,** "Computer Revolution." From Samuel F. O'Gorman, "Computer Revolution," *Senior Scholastic,* Vol. 115, No. 3, October 1, 1982. Reprinted by permission of Scholastic Inc. **Abigail Jungreis,** "Revolution in the Workplace." From *Scholastic Update,* Vol. 116, No. 1, September 2, 1983. Reprinted by permission of Scholastic Inc. **Peter H. Wagschal,** "A Last Chance for Computers in the Schools?" From Peter H. Wagschal, "A Last Chance for Computers in the Schools?" *Phi Delta Kappan,* December 1984. Reprinted by permission. **Franz-Olivier Giesbert,** "The Computer Fallacy." From an interview with Joseph Weizenbaum entitled "The Computer Fallacy." Copyright © 1984 by *Harper's* Magazine. Reprinted from the March 1984 issue by special permission. The article originally appeared in *Le Nouvel Observateur,* December 2, 1983. **Neil Chayet,** "When Eating Out Is Against the Law," "The Best Interests of the Child," "After Divorce, Where Do All the Children Go?" "What's

Credits continue on page 278.

For Linda and Richard
R. L. S.

To Casey and Justin, with appreciation for their support and encouragement
J. M. K.

Contents

Preface

Milestones is an intermediate-level language text for students of English as a foreign language that provides readings and exercises as a source and stimulus for student understanding and production of English. It assumes that the essential conditions for the learning of a second language include the presentation of significant amounts of interesting material in that language and a variety of opportunities to use it.

The text presents thirty-six contemporary readings, mostly nonfiction, arranged thematically into nine chapters. Each chapter has four related readings, beginning with a short reading from 300–750 words long, a core reading of about 750–1,000 words, and two supplementary readings. Topics include personal relationships, challenges of nature and technology, the law, social and economic problems, health, and work. The readings are taken from contemporary newspapers, magazines, and books, and represent a variety of discourse: informal conversation; television talk; formal interview; informal prose, light and serious; formal prose; reports on science; literary writing. The original wording of the authors has generally been retained and some selections have been shortened. The chapters are self-contained and may be used in any order.

Milestones continues the focus of the lower-level *Stimulus* on leading students to read, talk, and write by giving them readings of contemporary interest and a rich variety of exercises that require the use of English while involving their memory, intellect, and curiosity. This text emphasizes (1) vocabulary expansion and (2) controlled to free speaking and writing activities. Intermediate-level students often feel frustrated at their learning rate, and the language activities here, among other things, call attention to new vocabulary, offer expanded contexts for many of the new vocabulary items, and provide a good deal of practice in the use of these items. The acquisition of vocabulary at this level builds confidence and gives a sense of progress. The many directed writing activities then provide the opportunities to use what has been learned.

Each reading is preceded by some background information and several brief questions, usually directed at the students' own experiences, often calling attention to a key word that is significant for the point of the reading. Although this preparation is sufficient for many intermediate classes, for others at a lower level of proficiency, instructors like to expand this activity by introducing a fuller vocabulary check before the reading. The readings are followed by a *Comprehension* exercise which includes both informational and inferential questions. The *Discussion* section then introduces questions that raise implications and relate the topic to student experience; this section can form the basis for significant conversational and argumentative interaction in class (the *Applications* exercise fulfills the function of the *Discussion* section for the initial readings). The *Language Practice* section contains a variety of exercises: a good number of them are vocabulary exercises that provide reenforcement and extended contexts for items in the reading: students associate word and context in rewriting and matching activities and then they use the words productively in fill-in and freer writing activities. In addition to the vocabulary work, there is a wide variety of controlled, directed, and free speaking and writing activities at the sentence and paragraph level. Sections entitled *Topics for Further Discussion or Writing* and *Follow-up Activities* require students to 1) reflect and report on their own attitudes and experiences, 2) find out information by talking to classmates and reporting that information, and 3) find information outside of the classroom by going to sources or talking to people and then report on their experiences.

In recognition of the broad range of proficiencies encountered in intermediate-level classes, the exercises vary in level of difficulty. For example, in one frequent and rather structured exercise, students are asked to look at a list of words taken from the reading and fit them into spaces provided in a paragraph on a similar topic. Another exercise, however, gives them new sentences with underlined vocabulary items that they may or may not know and asks them to find an equivalent for the items in a particular paragraph in the reading; many students may already know the underlined items (their level of difficulty is below that of the items in the reading) and others will realize the meaning when they compare the contexts, but if the class level is low, the instructor may preface the exercise by having the students look up any new words in a dictionary. Similarly, some writing exercises demand a fairly controlled response: students may be asked to summarize one paragraph in one sentence, and they can do this using structures and vocabulary they are very comfortable with. But a sentence combination exercise requires them to produce structures they may not normally use; again, if the class level is low, the instructor might take advantage of the exercise to review grammatical structures.

It should also be noted that there are many ways to work with this material. Many of the exercises can be done orally or in writing. They can also be done in a variety of contexts: student to student and student to teacher in class; student alone in class; student to outsider and outsider to student out of class; student alone out of class. Thus the material may be used in both 1) integrated programs, where the class focus is on communication, and 2) skill programs, especially for components devoted to speaking-writing, reading, writing, and reading-writing.

Acknowledgments

We would like to express our appreciation to our reviewers, Ben Bernanke of Princeton University, Bruce R. Bolnick of Northeastern University, Joe Brocato of North Texas State University, Patricia Byrd of Georgia State University, Donald H. Dutkowsky of Syracuse University, Merton D. Finkler of Lawrence University, Mary Fish of University of Alabama, John A. Flanders of Central Methodist College, John W. Graham of University of Illinois at Champaign–Urbana, Kathryn Hanges of Concordia College, Stanley Kaish of Rutgers University–Newark, Benjamin J.C. Kim of University of Nebraska–Lincoln, Tryphon Kollintzas of University of Pittsburgh, Lori Roberts Liner of Wayne State University, Jeffrey B. Miller of University of Delaware, G. Michael Phillips of California State University at Northridge, Andrew J. Policano of University of Iowa, Alan Rabin of University of Tennessee, Robert H. Rasche of Michigan State University, H. David Robison of Louisiana Tech University, Michael K. Salemi of University of North Carolina at Chapel Hill, Pamela J. Sharpe, Jean Mullen Smith of Northeastern University, James A. Wilcox of University of California at Berkeley, and to Nancy Benjamin and the editorial staff at Little, Brown. Very special thanks go to Francine Stieglitz, who contributed so much to the plan of the text and the choice of selections.

Milestones | **1**

Milestones are important events in a person's life. In this chapter, four people write about times in their lives when something important happened to them, something that they didn't forget.

Fear

Before You Read

Gordon Lish, who writes short stories and novels, teaches writing at Columbia University. In "Fear," we have the first two examples from his short story "Fear: Four Examples." Here he describes some of the fears that a person experiences when he or she reaches the milestone of parenthood.

Think About It

Have you ever been responsible for others (people or animals) and worried about them?

About what aspect of your life do (or did) your parents worry most?

Fear

Gordon Lish

My daughter called from college. She is a good student, excellent grades, is gifted in any number of ways.

"What time is it?" she said.

I said, "It is two o'clock."

"All right," she said. "It's two now. Expect me at four — four by the clock that said it's two."

"It was my watch," I said.

"Good," she said.

It is ninety miles, an easy drive.

At a quarter to four, I went down to the street. I had these things in mind — look for her car, hold a parking place, be there waving when she turned into the block.

At a quarter to five, I came back up.

I changed my shirt. I wiped off my shoes. I looked into the mirror to see if I looked like someone's father.

She presented herself shortly after six o'clock.

"Traffic?" I said.

"No," she said, and that was the end of that.

After supper, she complained of insufferable pains, and doubled over on the dining-room floor.

"My belly," she said.

"What?" I said.

She said, "My belly. It's agony. Get me a doctor."

There is a large and famous hospital mere blocks from my apartment. Celebrities go there, statesmen, people who must know what they are doing.

With the help of a doorman and an elevator man, I got my daughter to the hospital. Within minutes, two physicians and a corps of nurses took the matter in hand.

I stood by watching.

It was hours and hours before they had her undoubled and were willing to announce their findings.

A bellyache . . .

Comprehension

Expand your understanding of the story's main ideas.

1. What did the father think was the danger for the daughter in the first example?

2. Why did the father look in the mirror? What do you think he saw in the mirror?

3. Why was the daughter late?

4. What could the father do when his daughter was in the hospital?

Applications

Relate the story to events in your own life.

1. Tell or write about a time when you did something that worried your family.

2. Describe an experience when you had to go to a doctor or hospital.

3. What do you think of the daughter's attitude about her arrival time?

My First Car

Before You Read

In this interview Wilt Chamberlain, a well-known former basketball player, tells about his experiences with his first car. His language is very informal and he uses contemporary expressions such as "really cool" and "make these moves."

Think About It

Do you know any sixteen- or seventeen-year-olds who own their own cars? What do they use their cars for?

Do you remember the first car in which you rode without your parents?

My First Car

Wilt Chamberlain

1 "My first car was a 1949 black Oldsmobile — the one with the slanted back, not the one with just the humped back. I always thought that Oldsmobiles were fast, and being a 16-year-old kid, I liked fast cars. I was able to purchase the car with the savings I had from working as a bellhop at a country club. I was the first person in my family to own a car.

2 "I never got into putting a lot of ornaments on the car to make it look jazzy. I always thought that detracted from it. What I did, though,

was put on one of those steering-wheel knobs so I could drive with one hand and look really cool.

3   "In the morning I had a regular route. I'd start with my sister Barbara, who went to school with me, and later my younger sister Yvonne. Then Barbara had a girlfriend I would pick up. After that I'd get Vinson Miller, who was my best friend at the time, and then pick up another guy named Biddy. Oh, we had a carload, always with three or four girls. You'd be amazed at how many people could get into that car.

4   "No, it was not too early for dating. But it might have been too early for the girls, because they were saying no more than they were saying yes, I'll tell you that. But my friend and I, we kept trying. We were cruisers. In most cases we ended up cruising with our sisters and their girlfriends, but we were out there. We'd find these streets where we knew certain young ladies lived, and after basketball practice on Saturdays we'd make these moves up and down the streets. I'm not sure what they thought of us, whether we were being foolish, cool, or whatever, but in most cases, it was all such innocent fun that everyone would just wave and say, 'Hi! What are you doing here?' And we'd say, 'Oh, we're just on our way to pick up a Christmas tree,' or something.

5   "What happened to the car was a shame. It was August, and I was on my way to the University of Kansas. I was going to trade in this car for a new one — a 1955 Oldsmobile — and I was going to roll into Kansas a really cool college kid. I was coming from visiting my sister in the Poconos, and I ran into a hurricane early in the morning. The winds were gusting and blowing like you would not believe, and my tires were about as bald as the haircut I was wearing at the time. One gust took the car for a bit of a spin off the side of the road. It hit two telegraph poles and the side of a tree and turned over about four times. I didn't have anything but a scratch on my head, but the only thing left of the car was that knob I had put on the steering wheel.

6   "The junk people offered me $24.50 for the remains of my car, and the towing service wanted to charge me $26 to tow it. It was a $1.50 deficit, and being fairly good in math, you understand, I left it there, with tears in my eyes."

Comprehension

1. Why did Wilt Chamberlain get an Oldsmobile?

2. What kind of ornaments did Chamberlain put on his car? Did he like ornaments on the car?

3. Approximately how many people did he usually take in his car?

4. What did he use his first car for?

5. Do you think his family was wealthy? Why or why not?

6. What happened to the car?

7. Why did he leave the car?

8. What kind of haircut did he have?

9. What do you think *cool* means here?

10. What do you think *cruisers* means?

Discussion

1. How important are cars for young people in your country?

2. Chamberlain wanted to impress the students at the University of Kansas with his car. What are some other ways in which young people try to impress others?

3. Why do you think there are so many car accidents?

Language Practice

Find the meaning of the underlined words in the following sentences. Then rewrite each sentence, substituting appropriate words or phrases for the underlined ones.

1. I was able to purchase a car. _____

2. You'd be amazed at how many people could get into that car. _____

_____

3. We're just on our way to pick up a Christmas tree. _____

_____

4. The winds were gusting. _____

5. The junk people offered me $24.50. _____

_____

6. The towing service wanted to charge me $26.00. _____

_____

The following words may remind you of other words. List as many of these words as you can. The first one is an example.

1. fun *games, laugh, pleasure, amusing, parties* ⎯⎯⎯⎯⎯⎯⎯⎯

2. dating ⎯⎯⎯⎯⎯⎯⎯⎯⎯⎯⎯⎯⎯⎯⎯⎯⎯⎯⎯⎯⎯⎯⎯⎯⎯⎯⎯⎯⎯

3. foolish ⎯⎯⎯⎯⎯⎯⎯⎯⎯⎯⎯⎯⎯⎯⎯⎯⎯⎯⎯⎯⎯⎯⎯⎯⎯⎯⎯⎯

4. bald ⎯⎯⎯⎯⎯⎯⎯⎯⎯⎯⎯⎯⎯⎯⎯⎯⎯⎯⎯⎯⎯⎯⎯⎯⎯⎯⎯⎯⎯⎯

Choose the appropriate forms of the words in each set below and write them in the blanks.

1. regular   regularly   regularity

His mother had a ⎯⎯⎯⎯⎯⎯ route. Every morning she would ⎯⎯⎯⎯

pick up the girls — first Marcia, then Barbara, then Yvonne — and take them

to school. The other mothers appreciated her ⎯⎯⎯⎯⎯⎯ .

2. foolish   foolishly   foolishness

When young boys try to impress girls, they often act ⎯⎯⎯⎯⎯⎯ . Some-

times the girls laugh at this ⎯⎯⎯⎯⎯⎯ , and as a result the boys may

feel ⎯⎯⎯⎯⎯⎯ .

The following sentences are not in correct order. Write them in the correct order on the lines below.

When I graduated from Harvard in 1946 I bought another one.
Since my father had paid only $300.00 for it, I made $100.00.
The first car I owned was a 1940 Ford.
I kept it for two years and sold it for $400.00.
My father bought it for me in the summer of 1943.

⎯⎯⎯⎯⎯⎯⎯⎯⎯⎯⎯⎯⎯⎯⎯⎯⎯⎯⎯⎯⎯⎯⎯⎯⎯⎯⎯⎯⎯⎯⎯⎯⎯⎯

⎯⎯⎯⎯⎯⎯⎯⎯⎯⎯⎯⎯⎯⎯⎯⎯⎯⎯⎯⎯⎯⎯⎯⎯⎯⎯⎯⎯⎯⎯⎯⎯⎯⎯

_____

_____

_____

What questions were asked to get the following information? Write the questions on the blank lines in the left-hand column.

_____	It was a 1939 Dodge.
_____	My father bought it for me for $125.00.
_____	We would drive in the car and play music on the radio.
_____	I had it for six years.
_____	One night it was raining and we drove right off the road into a lake.
_____	It stopped in the middle of a field and I left it there.

Write a paragraph about a car or another object by answering the questions below.

When did you get your first (car)? How did you get it? Why did you get it? What did you use it for? What happened to it?

_____

_____

_____

_____

_____

_____

Combine phrases from Column A and Column B into sentences and write them below.

A	**B**
What I did was	so I could drive with one hand.
I never got the car to Kansas	that I would pick up.
I put on a steering-wheel knob	work as a bellhop in a country club.
My sister had a girlfriend	because I had an accident.
What happened to the car	for the girls to start dating.
It might have been too early	was a shame.

1. _____

2. _____

3. _____

4. _____

5. _____

6. _____

Choose your own words to fill in the blanks below.

My first _____ was a _____ . I got it in _____

when I was _____ . I got it from _____ . I brought it

to _____ , but _____ .

As a result, _____ .

Write a four- or five-sentence paragraph on the topic: My First _____

_____ .

_____

_____

_____

_____

_____

Follow-up Activities

1. Interview two people about something that was important to them when they were younger. Find out when they got it, what they did with it, what happened to it, and so on. Be ready to describe what you found out.

2. Choose something that you would like to have now. Find out where to get it and how much it costs. Imagine how it would change your life. Be ready to describe it.

Topics for Further Discussion and Writing

1. Why do you think young people like to drive cars fast?

2. As a youth, Chamberlain worked a lot. What do you think of the idea of young people working? Should all young people work? Should they receive the same pay as adults?

3. Chamberlain and his friends dated girls when they were sixteen. What do you think of U.S. dating customs? How do boys and girls get to know each other in your country?

4. Many car accidents are caused by drivers who have been drinking alcohol. Do you think there should be a law against the sale of alcohol to certain people? What are your country's laws about the sale of alcohol?

A Thanksgiving Memory

Before You Read

Once when Bob Greene was a young newspaper reporter living in Chicago, he couldn't go home to visit his family for the Thanksgiving holiday. In this selection he tells how he spent that Thanksgiving.

Think About It

Think of a time when you were away from home on an important holiday.

Do you know what animal crackers are?

A Thanksgiving Memory

Bob Greene

1   It was his first Thanksgiving away from home, and he thought it would be a good change, with the football games on television and none of the relatives to bother him and ask him how life in the big city was.

2   After all the years of dinners with the cousins and the aunts and uncles, he was looking forward to being by himself for once. This was just a couple of years ago, his first Thanksgiving out of college, and he was a reporter for a newspaper in an important city, and he didn't feel like going home.

3   So for the first time ever, he wouldn't be there. During the four college years, he had made the reservations so he could be in Ohio the day before, so he could be there and be bored on Thanksgiving night and wish he was back by himself. Not this time, though; this Thanksgiving would be just another day, which is how he wanted it.

4   So on Thanksgiving morning, he made the telephone call and told his family that yes, he was sorry he couldn't be there, too, and yes, he was missing them. But really he was happy that he wouldn't have to put up with it for once, and he sat back to ease it through the day.

5   He had bought some sliced turkey for dinner, which he thought was a nice irony. But about noon or a little after, he ate all the turkey up, and it was gone. And in the middle of the afternoon he was getting hungry and it was dark outside, and he didn't like being there so much anymore.

6   It was a one-room apartment in Rogers Park, what they call a modern studio. But all it was really was a 9-by-12 cubicle with white walls and a hallway leading off to a bathroom, for $135 a month. A 45-minute L ride away from the Loop, and by five o'clock he couldn't take it anymore. It hadn't got to the point where he wished he was with the uncles and cousins, but this certainly wasn't the way he wanted to spend his Thanksgiving.

7   By six o'clock, he knew he would have to have something to eat. He looked in the icebox, and all he had was a bottle of Spanada wine, bought for a buck a couple of days before. And in the cupboard there were two boxes of animal crackers, which made him laugh. He couldn't remember when he had bought those.

8   He knew that the grocery down the block usually stayed open until nine o'clock, so he walked down to get himself some hamburger

for dinner. He was really hungry by now, and ready for a quick meal and then an attempt at sleep, even though he wasn't tired.

9   But when he got to the store, it was closed — closed since four o'clock because it was Thanksgiving Day. No food after all. There was no one on the street, and he started to walk. He walked for about an hour, and the snow had begun to come, and yes, he was lonely. He even thought about being home.

10   He started back for his one-room apartment, so he could pull his hide-a-bed out and try for sleep. He passed the grocery store again, and the girl was there.

11   She was alone, too. She was wanting to buy some food, and she was just finding out that she could not, because today the store was closed.

12   Her name, it seems now, was Janie. She was wearing baggy blue-jeans and a pea jacket, and standing by the door of the closed store she looked sad and absolutely beautiful. He stopped to talk with her. This was her first Thanksgiving alone, too.

13   They stood in the snow for a while, and then they figured that this was silly. So they went up to his room for their Thanksgiving dinner.

14   It was a dinner of animal crackers and Spanada wine, and it was delicious. They ate it slowly, and they talked, and it was easier to smile than before.

15   She said that she had thought it would be easy to spend the day with herself, but when dinnertime came, she had felt the same sadness. And they both laughed because they were supposed to be old enough to stay above such feelings.

16   They laughed a lot that night, and the one room was warm and nice. And when the night was over, they both said that it was the best Thanksgiving they had ever had, and that they would like to see each other again. But they each knew it was a lie, although a lovely lie, and the girl named Janie went away, and now she is just a Thanksgiving memory.

17   It was only a couple of years ago. They never did see each other again. So he does not know what became of the girl named Janie, where she went or what she is doing. But it is Thanksgiving again, and he is hoping that she is having a happy one, maybe even the second best one ever.

Comprehension

1. Why did Bob Greene want to stay in the city on Thanksgiving Day?

2. How did he feel on Thanksgiving morning?

3. What was Janie doing when Bob first saw her?

4. What did they have for dinner?

5. What made them happy?

6. What was the lie that they told each other?

7. Did Bob and Janie see each other after that Thanksgiving?

Discussion

1. What were some of the things that probably made Bob feel so lonely on Thanksgiving?

2. Do you think that this is a happy memory for Bob Greene? Why or why not?

3. If you have been away from home on a holiday, how did you spend it?

Language Practice

Fill in the blanks in the paragraph below with words from this list:

away from	silly	spend
by	sad	bother
for	bored	laugh
through	lonely	
about		
on		
with		

It was Michael's first weekend _____ campus. He had finished his studying _____ Saturday afternoon and he had nothing to do. He was _____ . He walked _____ the library, where he saw a classmate reading, but he didn't want to _____ her. Then he saw another classmate, but she looked _____ and he wanted to be _____ someone who could make him _____ . So he waited outside the library _____ an hour, but no one came by. It was _____ six o'clock and he didn't know how he was going to _____ the evening. Life was _____ without friends.

Combine phrases from Column A and Column B into sentences and write them below.

A	**B**
He thought it would be a good change	how life in the big city was.
He told his family that	spending the holiday alone.
He wanted to have a good dinner	were two boxes of animal crackers.
He stopped to say something	but he didn't have much food in the house.
Janie didn't feel like	to spend Thanksgiving in Chicago.
He didn't want his relatives to ask him	he was sorry he couldn't be there.
All he had	even though he didn't know her.

1. _____

2. _____

3. _____

4. _____

5. _____

6. _____

7. _____

With which of the situations in the right-hand column can you associate the sentences below? Circle the correct answer in the right-hand column.

1. She didn't feel like going home.
   a. She was probably living away from home.
   b. She was probably happy about the idea of the trip.
   c. She was probably at home waiting for someone to call.

2. He was looking forward to being   a. He wanted to find his own
    by himself.   friend.
                                             b. He wanted to be alone.
                                             c. He was looking in a mirror.

3. By five o'clock he couldn't take   a. The store closed at five o'clock
    it anymore.   so he couldn't go back there.
                                             b. He was unhappy with what he
                                                 was doing and wanted to
                                                 change.
                                             c. He needed a lot of time to do
                                                 more work.

4. He was happy he wouldn't have   a. There was a heavy box and
    to put up with it.   someone had to lift it.
                                             b. There was noise and music and
                                                 arguments.
                                             c. There was a nice group of
                                                 people that he always enjoyed.

Write two or three sentences describing a phone call that you made (as in paragraph 4 of the story). Include what you said.

_____

_____

_____

Which holiday do you like best? Write three or four sentences to tell why.

_____

_____

_____

Describe the room or apartment in which you live. Tell about its size, the objects in it, and their arrangement. Include shapes and colors. Before you begin to write, you may want to refer to that part of the story describing the young man's room.

_____

_____

_____

Follow-up Activities

1. Discover what people usually have for Thanksgiving dinner.

2. Find out the holiday on which your classmates or friends especially want to be with their families. Ask why they chose those holidays.

3. Ask a friend or classmate to tell you about a surprising incident that happened when he or she was away from home for the first time. Compare stories with those collected by other class members.

_____

The First Day of the War

Before You Read

"The First Day of the War" is the opening chapter of *Till the Break of Day*, in which Maia Wojciechowska describes her experience as a child during World War II. In this selection, she remembers her thoughts as she used to watch her father in his plane. Then she describes the coming of another plane that started the war for her.

Think About It

Have you heard or read anything that describes the effects of war on children?

Do you know anyone whose pet was killed when he or she was young?

The First Day of the War

Maia Wojciechowska

1 It started like the best of all mornings. I woke up from a dream to the sound of the plane.

2   He would often come early in the morning, and I always knew he

would not land before I got out of bed and ran outside. While waiting, he would make lazy circles in the sky. And as I rushed out, there would always be an unasked question in my mind: did he love fear more than freedom or freedom more than fear? For he always did something frightening that might end his freedom: rolls and spins and that horrible, inevitable climb into the infinity of the sky. Each time I saw him go vertically away from me, I thought he wouldn't *want* to come down.

3   But he always did. And that descent, straight down, the nose of the plane an arrow shooting the earth, falling, gaining in loudness as he lost altitude, made me catch my breath and forced my eyes to close. Would he straighten up in time? Would a wing catch a treetop as it once did? But he was immortal. The plane might lose a wing or even burn, but nothing would happen to him. Not to my hero, my flying knight, my father.

4   Even as I raced against the landing plane, trying to reach it before he cut the engine, hoping that he would have time to take me up, trying not to be blown down by the great gusts of wind from the propeller blades, even as I climbed up to the cockpit, I was afraid. Afraid that he would be alone, unreachable, private in that world of his where I couldn't even be a trespasser. Even flying with him, beside him, even then he was still a fugitive from me.

5   Today was different. The sound of the plane was gone by the time I rushed outside. Then I heard another. Not just one but several planes were flying overhead. Next to me was my newest possession, one he had not yet seen — a Doberman puppy. The dog had no name yet. He was brand new, and I loved him. Yesterday, when I got him, he had run away from the vet who was going to trim his ears and cut his tail to a stump. The litter of five submitted yappingly to the operation, but not he. He tore himself away from me, and I chased him through a swamp, across what I was afraid was a bed of quicksand, wanting to catch him and yet also wanting him to get away. Now his black glistening body, for he had fallen into a puddle, was jumping over weeds and disappearing into the tall grass.

6   Now there was another plane. I looked up, but it wasn't his — it did not have white and red squared under the wings. The plane dipped down and flew low, parallel with my running dog. It slid down even lower, and there was a sound — a sound I didn't understand, a sound I had never heard before. As my dog leaped up, I saw him for a brief moment over the grass, shadowed by the plane's wing. Then the plane rose and flew away.

7   I stood in that field not moving, waiting for my dog to continue running in that sunlit place, which was at the edge of my summer world, but I couldn't see him anywhere. And there were no sounds — not one single sound since that sound that I was now beginning to understand. As I started to walk forward, I already knew what I would see, and knowing was evil and I wanted to take back what I knew.

8   I did not bury my dog. I did not touch him. I turned away from him because he did not move. He would never have a name.

9   I climbed a tree and sat there, trying not to think of anything, trying not to hate. But trying did no good and I hated — everything I knew and everything that I didn't understand. I hated everyone, especially those who now were making noises inside my house. I hated the car that had pulled in front of the house and its running, sputtering engine. And most of all I hated my mother's voice calling my name and the slamming of the doors. And I hated the summer for having so suddenly ended.

10   When I got tired of hating, I came down off the tree and swore to myself that nobody would ever know what had happened to my dog. I promised not to say anything to anyone, not until I understood why and who had done it. Not until I found a way of paying them back. Not until after I killed the one who had killed him.

Comprehension

1. Who would often come early in the morning?

2. What question did Maia ask herself when she watched her father's plane? Why did she ask that question?

3. What was her attitude toward her father?

4. How long did she have her dog? What were some of the things that the dog did?

5. What was the sound that she had never heard before? What happened to the dog?

6. How did she react to the dog's death?

Discussion

1. How important do you think this incident was in the life of the author?

2. Have you had experiences in which you learned something important about the nature of the world?

3. What was your reaction to this reading? How did it make you feel?

Language Practice

Find words or phrases in the reading that have meanings similar to those words and phrases underlined below. Then rewrite the sentences using words or phrases from the reading.

1. As I <u>hurried outside</u>, there would always be an unasked question in my mind. (See paragraph 2.)

   _____

   _____

2. But he <u>would never die</u>. (See paragraph 3.)

   _____

   _____

3. Not just one but <u>a few</u> planes were flying overhead. (See paragraph 5.)

   _____

   _____

4. I chased him through a swamp, wanting to catch him and wanting him to <u>escape</u>. (See paragraph 5.)

   _____

   _____

5. As my dog <u>jumped up</u>, I saw him for a <u>short time</u> over the grass. (See paragraph 6.)

   _____

   _____

6. The plane <u>went up</u> and flew away. (See paragraph 6.)

   _____

   _____

7. And I hated the summer for having so <u>quickly</u> ended. (See paragraph 9.)

   _____

   _____

Combine phrases from Column A and Column B into sentences and write them below in paragraph form. Be sure to put them into a logical order.

A	**B**
I wanted to know	trying not to hate.
I turned away from my dog	pay them back.
Then I climbed into a tree and sat there	who had done it and why they did it.
Then I was going to	everyone and everything I knew.
But I hated	because he didn't move.
When I finished hating, I promised	everything I didn't understand.
And I hated	not to say anything to anyone.

_____

_____

_____

_____

_____

_____

_____

_____

Match the words below in Column A to the appropriate situation in Column B and write a sentence describing that situation.

EXAMPLE: 1. frightening   _1_   The girl was afraid of the noises made by the warplanes and the guns.

1. *The sounds of the war were frightening to the girl.*

A	B
1. brief	_____ She wanted to live in her own world without sharing it with other people.
2. lazy	
3. fear	_____ The little girl watched as the pilot of the airplane killed her dog.
4. inevitable	_____ She didn't want to get out of bed and go to school; she didn't want to do anything.
5. private	
6. horrible	_____ She had her dog for only one day.
	_____ They knew that the war was going to change their lives, and there was nothing they could do about it.
	_____ They were so frightened by the planes that they wouldn't leave their home.

1. _____

2. _____

3. _____

4. _____

5. _____

6. _____

Write two or three sentences describing an activity that your father (or another relative) used to do when you were young. Begin: "When I was young, my . . . would . . ."

_____

_____

_____

Watching her father's plane was a frightening experience for the young girl. Write two or three sentences describing a frightening experience that you have had.

_____

_____

_____

Follow-up Activities

1. Interview your classmates about the first time they heard about a war. Ask questions such as: What is the first war that you remember? How did you hear about it? What was your reaction? Compare their answers.

2. Ask your friends or relatives the question: What was the most unpleasant surprise you have ever had? Compare answers.

3. Collect information about World War II. Who was fighting against whom? How long did it last? In what countries did it take place?

4. Find the book *Till the Break of Day* and discover what happened to Maia during the war.

Chapter Review

1. Both Lish and Wojciechowska write about fear. How are their fears different?

2. All of the authors wrote about an incident or experience in their lives that was significant for them. Choose an incident in your life (for example, losing someone or something, a first responsibility, an act of kindness or cruelty, and so on). Be prepared to tell or write about it.

3. Which of these authors would you like to read more of? Tell why.

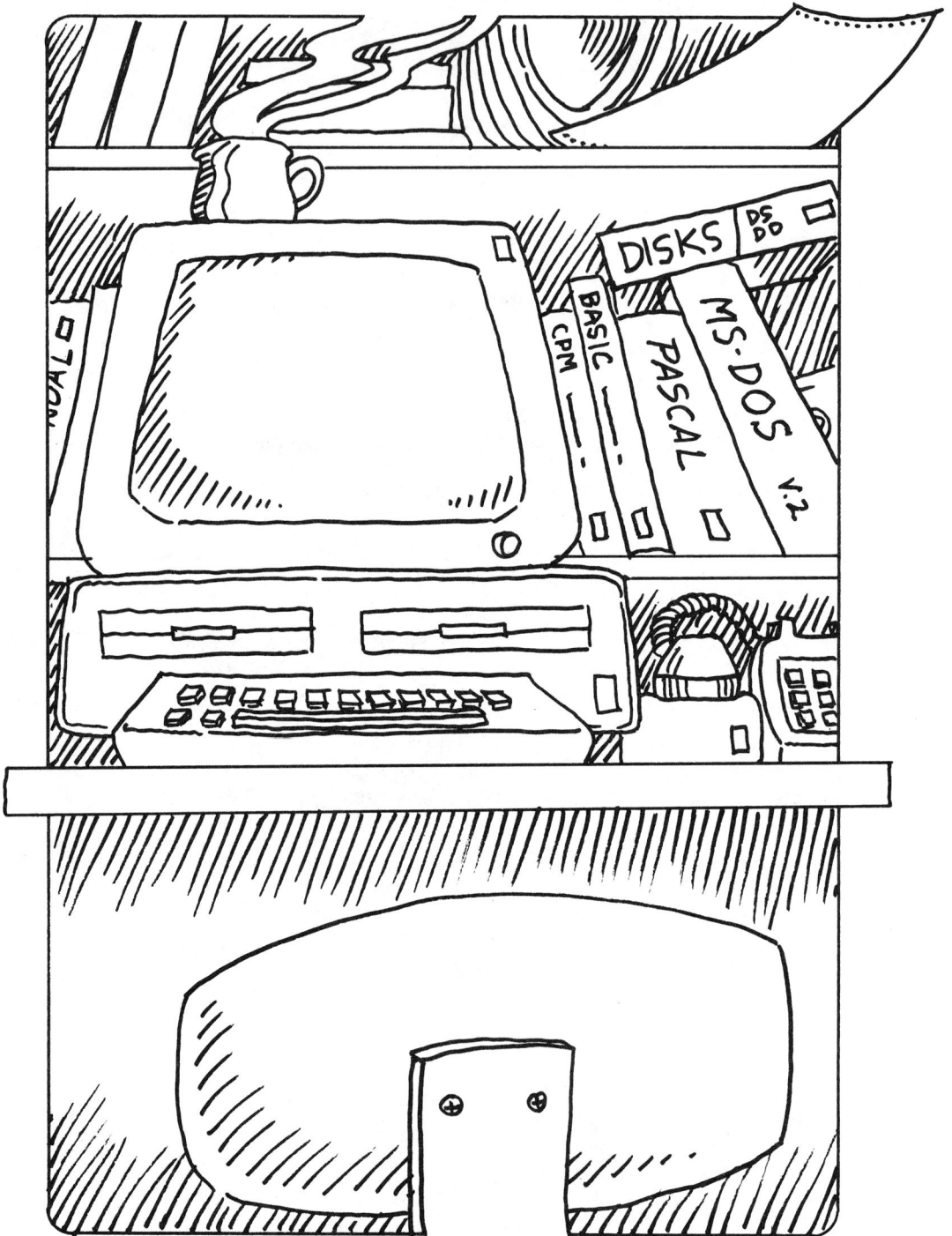

Servants or Masters?

2

Are computers our servants or our masters? The authors of the readings in this chapter discuss how we can and should use computers; they also call our attention to what computers cannot do.

Computer Revolution

Before You Read

This reading describes some jobs for which computers are used and some attitudes that people have developed toward computers.

Think About It

How important are computers for you in your studies?

Identify a job now usually done with the help of computers. How was it done before computers? Have computers benefited those who use them?

Computer Revolution

Samuel F. O'Gorman

1　Computers are now being used to direct traffic in the sky, find minerals in the soil, control robots at work, track stars in the heavens, diagnose diseases, analyze chemicals, and make movies.

2   "We are living in a computer society . . . ," a school superintendent recently remarked. That fact delights some people. It angers others. But two developments within the past five years have greatly increased public awareness of computers. One was the development of low-cost microcomputers. That put computers into thousands of classrooms, homes and small businesses. The other development was the widespread introduction of video games.

3   Coin-operated video games, beeping, buzzing and blinking in donut shops, candy stores, game rooms, pizza restaurants and laundromats introduce many people to computer concepts. These games have helped a whole generation of young people feel at home with computers. Most students today do not consider learning computer skills a "big deal."

4   With many older people, however, video games have given computers a bad name. Use of personal computers for games has added to the misconceptions about computers. People need to be assured that computers are not all fun and games. They also need to be assured that a person doesn't have to be a programming expert to be a competent computer user.

5   One young computer consultant exlained, "Computers are just tools . . . there's nothing secret or special about them." A computer can't do anything on its own. A computer doesn't do anything that isn't fed into it by a user. As with any tool, a user needs to learn to do certain jobs with a computer.

6   Computers are useful tools because they can process information at an extremely rapid rate. A small computer can do calculations faster than a roomful of accountants. A big computer can do them faster than a town full of accountants.

7   A computer is also useful because it has an excellent memory — it can store vast amounts of information. A computer chip circuit no bigger than a postage stamp can hold the contents of a book. And information can be drawn out of a computer's vast memory in a fraction of a second. For instance, a person can now walk up to a bank teller and learn the balance of his/her checking account in less than a minute. Before the computer age, the person would most likely be told to wait for a statement at the end of the month. With the help of an encyclopedia in a computer memory, a librarian can provide information in a few minutes that might have taken days of research before the computer age.

8   The use of general purpose computers and of specialized computer circuits (microprocessors) in various devices has made life easier for many people. It has also greatly increased the amount of work a person can do.

9   As computers are used more and more at work, at school and at home, the benefits will be enormous. But there will also be stresses and dislocations. As some jobs are eliminated, people will have to be retrained for new jobs. Social scientists point out that leaders of gov-

ernment, business and industry will have to see that people are retrained for the new technologies in a way that will make them feel
comfortable with those technologies.

Comprehension

Expand your understanding of the main ideas in the reading.

1. How did the development of low-cost microcomputers increase the public's
   awareness of computers?

2. What were some effects of the popularity of video games?

3. What are some of the misconceptions that adults have about computers?

4. Why are computers so useful?

5. What are some effects of computers?

Applications

Relate the reading to events in your own life.

1. If you are familiar with computers, describe how you learned to work with
   them: Where did you use them? Who helped you? What did you use them
   for?

2. Why do you think the increasing importance of computers delights some
   people and angers others?

3. Children seem very comfortable with computers. They are used to TV
   screens, and "the computer is a screen that responds to them, hooked to a
   machine that can be programmed to respond the way they want it to. That
   is power" (*Time*, January 3, 1983, p. 23). Do you agree that this is one of
   the computer's attractions for children? Why?

Revolution in the Workplace

Before You Read

Abigail Jungreis, a reporter for *Scholastic Update* magazine, visited factories
and offices in Delaware and New York to find out how computer technology is
changing work in the United States.

Think About It

What kind of work is being done with the help of computers?

What are some effects of computer use in offices and factories?

Revolution in the Workplace

Abigail Jungreis

1   Four years ago, Chuck Wilson spent his workday welding car sides to their underbodies. Today, computer-directed robots do the job, and Wilson makes sure that those robots don't break down.

2   Toni Catalano studied stenography and typing in secretarial school. But few people use stenography in the office where she works today. Instead, Catalano operates a word-processing machine that can figure accounts and correct typing errors.

3   What's happening in today's offices and factories? The answer is new computer technology. Only 15 years ago, most computers were big and very expensive. Then, in the 1970s, engineers figured out ways to get more and more information onto tiny chips made of silicon. Today, silicon chips are the brain cells of computers that can perform thousands of operations in a second — for a lot less than the old computers.

4   The new generation of small, cheap computers has invaded the workplace. Attached to telephones, computers can remember numbers and take messages. Computers can also be used to program the movement of a mechanical arm, creating a robot. These new machines mean big changes for workers.

COMPUTERS IN FACTORIES

5   At a Chrysler assembly plant in Newark, Delaware, the big change came in 1980. The company spent $50 million to update the plant's equipment. Included were more than 60 robots at $100,000 apiece.

6   In 1979, Chuck Wilson worked with 29 other people, welding sides on 60 cars an hour. Now, with only two other technicians, he watches robots put 70 car frames together in that time.

7   Wilson gets $2.50 an hour more than assembly-line workers. But the robots he watches save Chrysler a lot of money. They increase *productivity*, the amount each worker produces in an hour. Higher productivity lowers the cost of making a car.

8   Donald Coefield, personnel administrator at the factory, thinks there's a bigger benefit. "If the robot does 56 welds on a car," he explains, "you will get 56 identical welds on every car, every day." Robots, says Coefield, improve the *quality* of the product.

9   For Chuck Wilson, robots improved the quality of his job. Work-

ing in "the jungle," the nickname for the factory's body shop, Wilson used to get his glasses pitted and his clothes burned by flying sparks. His new job required a technical background and six weeks in robot school. "It's interesting," he says. "Something different." And he doesn't have to work in a shower of sparks anymore.

10   The U.S. has long been the leader in robot technology. Until recently, however, few robots made their way into U.S. factories. Japan's success in introducing "steel-collar" workers has changed that — especially in U.S. auto factories. Today, more than 5,000 robots work in U.S. manufacturing. And one study predicts that between 1980 and 1985, one out of five auto-assembly jobs will go to a robot.

11   Most of the robots on the job are blind and stupid. If the part they work on is not in the same position each time, they can't do their job.

12   A new generation of robots may soon be introduced into U.S. factories. Sensitive to light and sound, they can "see" and "hear" the pieces they put together. Experts predict that, eventually, robots will do 75 percent of all factory work.

13   Will robots put a lot of factory workers out of jobs — permanently? Not necessarily. Many factory workers can be retrained, the way Chuck Wilson was, to service the new machines. And computers may open up whole new industries. The greatest job-saver, though, may be the robots' ability to increase productivity. High productivity, by cutting costs, makes U.S. products more competitive. And that keeps U.S. industry in business.

COMPUTERS IN OFFICES

14   Still, the number of manufacturing jobs will continue to drop. More people will move from factory to office work. What will jobs there be like?

In 1977, Texaco, Inc. moved its executive offices 30 miles north, from New York City to Harrison, New York. The company installed the latest computerized equipment in the new offices — and boosted productivity. Before computer technology, they needed one secretary for every three executives. Now, one secretary supports five people.

15   The main reason behind the change is that secretaries don't use typewriters anymore. Instead, they have word processors. The secretaries type letters and reports into a computer that puts their words on a screen. If they catch their mistakes, they can correct them before the computer types anything up. They can even make changes later. The secretary just calls the letter back on the screen, makes the correction, and has it reprinted. The entire report doesn't have to be retyped by hand.

16   Word processors do more than just type. The IBM machine that Toni Catalano works on keeps accounts, does math, and even files electronically. "It can do everything," says Catalano.

17   Computerized equipment has made all kinds of office workers more productive. The mail at Texaco is delivered by a robot-run cart.

People in the mailroom load the cart. From then on, it travels around the offices without human assistance. Beeping a "hello," the cart stops at certain spots to let people load and unload its trays.

18   Computers save time for Texaco's executives. Instead of writing out or dictating a letter to a secretary, businessmen can call a special number. No matter where they're calling from, the number hooks them into a machine at the office that records the dictation. A secretary takes it off the machine and types it up.

19   Computers can send press releases and legal documents quickly to Texaco offices around the country. Experts predict that, in the future, most information will be sent through computers, not the post office.

20   Today's computerized office equipment has its limits. This article was written on a word processor — until the computer accidentally turned off. The computer didn't have time to store everything that was on the screen, and several paragraphs of the story were lost. Power shortages can wipe out files of material and make some work impossible.

21   But the biggest problem isn't electronic. Ralph Mandia, chief of Texaco's support services, says that many workers feel uncomfortable with the new technology. "Getting people to use it is like pulling teeth," he complains.

22   There will be even bigger adjustments in the future. "Eventually," Mandia predicts, "secretaries — if they're still called secretaries — will have all the files, statistics, and electronic mail available at their desks. And so will their bosses."

23   One thing is certain. As computer-run machines fill more jobs, possibilities for unskilled workers will dry up. There will be a greater demand for people with the know-how to take care of computers. "You don't have to spend four years in college," says Donald Coefield about the people he hires to maintain Chrysler's robots. "But you need technical training."

24   Still, Ralph Mandia, at Texaco, worries that basic skills may be lost in the rush for computer training. "Word processors can correct spelling," he explains. "But still, it's not the whole answer." Workers have to express themselves clearly and correctly. "That's something that has not changed, and will never change," claims Mandia.

25   Some experts think that computers may make office work out of date. "In 20 years," says Professor Margarethe Olsen, "a significant number of us will work at home, using computers and dealing with our offices by electronic mail."

26   Other experts worry that computers will make work less pleasant for humans. "Smart" robots may leave only boring, low-paying jobs for assembly-line workers. Word processors can record exactly how much work each operator is doing — and report the record to the supervisor. Government professor Alan Westin warns that "new technology may be an opportunity to grip workers totally."

27   Right now, it's hard to predict what tomorrow's workplace will be like. "We're only at the beginning," Ralph Mandia admits. The new

technology will create a different office in the future. "But when that's going to happen, and how it's going to happen," Mandia shrugs, "no one seems to know."

Comprehension

1. What is the revolution in the workplace described in the reading?

2. What are the benefits of using robots on an assembly line?

3. In what way are robots blind and stupid?

4. How does computerization change the nature of office work?

5. What are some problems created by increased use of computers in offices?

6. Which of the sentences below would best complete the following paragraph?

   Robots and computers do the jobs of many unskilled workers. Robots can weld cars, and computers can keep accounts and file. But new jobs may be created by computer technology as well. . . .

   a. For example, secretaries can make corrections without retyping a letter.
   b. Many factory workers will be out of work permanently.
   c. For example, workers will be needed to maintain the robots.

Discussion

1. How might the increasing use of computers affect your future?

2. What might happen to people who lose jobs because of computer technology?

3. What are some boring or dangerous jobs that could be done by robots?

Language Practice

Find the meaning of the underlined words in the following sentences. Then rewrite each sentence, substituting appropriate words or phrases for the underlined ones.

1. The cart <u>travels</u> around the office without human <u>assistance</u>. (See paragraph 17.)

2. Computers can <u>perform</u> thousands of operations per second. (See paragraph 3.)

_____

_____

3. <u>Cutting</u> costs makes products more competitive. (See paragraph 13.)

_____

4. One secretary <u>supports</u> five people. (See paragraph 14.)

_____

5. The <u>entire</u> report doesn't have to be retyped by hand. (See paragraph 15.)

_____

6. The cart stops at certain <u>spots</u> to let people load its trays. (See paragraph 17.)

_____

7. There will be a great demand for people with the <u>know-how</u> to take care of computers. (See paragraph 23.)

_____

_____

Substitute a word or phrase from the following list for an underlined word or phrase in the sentences below and rewrite the sentences.

| destroy | at work | connects | become useless |
| disappear | without work | old-fashioned | it makes no difference |

1. <u>No matter</u> where they're calling from, the computer <u>hooks</u> them into a machine at the office.

_____

_____

2. Will robots leave a lot of factory workers <u>out of jobs</u>?

_____

3. Computers may make office work <u>out of date</u>.

_____

4. Wilson makes sure that those robots don't <u>break down</u>.

_____

5. Most of the robots <u>on the job</u> are blind and stupid.

_____

6. Power shortages can <u>wipe out</u> files of materials.

_____

7. Possibilities for unskilled workers will <u>dry up</u>.

_____

Fill in the blanks below with a noun or verb from this list. You may use a word more than once.

Nouns		**Verbs**	
quality	equipment	perform	program
benefits	operations	install	maintain
productivity	machines	update	figure out
adjustments	limits		

In this article, Jungreis describes some of the _____ of computeri-

zation. She writes that workers will be able to _____ their jobs faster

and more easily. Also, the _____ of the _____ and the _____

_____ of the workers will increase. But there may be problems. Computers are only _____ and someone has to _____ how to operate a machine. In addition, when the machines arrive in an office, someone has to _____ them and make _____ . Since the machines are complicated, someone has to _____ them and, after a while, as a result of new technology, someone has to _____ them.

Computerized _____ is efficient, but it has its _____ .

In each set below, choose the appropriate forms of the words and write them in the blanks.

1. computer   computerize   computerization

    The Walsh Plumbing Equipment Company decided to _____ its delivery system. The _____ was programmed with information about routes and distances. But the _____ of the system didn't work very well: the programmer had used old maps.

2. productivity   produce   productive

    The use of computers may increase a company's _____ : a secretary may now _____ more work in less time. But the secretary may not continue to be _____ because working with a machine is boring.

3. correct   correction

    Computers can now _____ your spelling. You can type a paper, and the machine will make sure that all the spellings are _____ .

But the _____ of spellings may not be enough; can the machine

_____ ideas?

Combine the sentences below by following the directions for each set. Try to eliminate as many words as possible without changing the main ideas. Use pronouns where appropriate. Do not use a dictionary.

EXAMPLE: Toni studied stenography in secretarial school. Toni studied typing in secretarial school. (Use *and*.)

Toni studied stenography and typing in secretarial school.

1. The secretary worked with a computer. He completed 200 statements in one hour. (Use an —*ing* form.)

    _____

    _____

2. You can correct your mistakes easily. You can find your mistakes. (Use *if*.)

    _____

3. The computer prints letters. The computer keeps records. The computer does math. (Eliminate words; use *and*.)

    _____

    _____

4. The robot moves from room to room. The robot does not have any human assistance. (Use *without*.)

    _____

    _____

5. Word processors can't express ideas clearly. Word processors can correct spelling. (Use *but*.)

    _____

    _____

Note the meaning of the phrase *out of date*. On the lines below, describe something that has become out of date and tell what has replaced it.

_____

_____

_____

_____

_____

The author writes that some robots are *sensitive* to light and sound. Find the meaning of *sensitive*. Write one or two sentences describing things to which you are sensitive.

_____

_____

"The company installed the *latest* computerized equipment in the new office." What does *latest* mean? What could you describe as "the latest"? Write the description below.

_____

_____

"The *main* reason behind the change is that secretaries don't use typewriters anymore." The *main reason* is the most important reason. Identify a change and describe the main reason for it below.

_____

_____

Note the use of *few* in this sentence: "Few people use stenography in the office." Remember that *few* has a negative meaning — not many. *A few* means some.

EXAMPLES: The computer was not a success: few people bought it.

                The new computer had a few problems, but the
                programmer solved them quickly.

Using the vocabulary in each set below, write two sentences with *few* and two sentences with *a few*.

1. secretaries   typewriters   office   nowadays

_____

2. computer   problems   programmer   solved

_____

3. learn   operate   computer   weeks

_____

4. people   comfortable   office   full   machines

_____

Using information from the reading, complete the following paragraph in your own words.

Years ago, automobile factories needed many workers. _____

_____

_____

Today, _____

_____

In your own words, complete the following paragraph by describing some process or activity that has changed in recent years.

Years ago, _____

_____

Today, _____

_____

Describe two benefits of using computers in the workplace.

_____

_____

_____

Follow-up Activities

1. Find out (from a computer magazine or someone who works with computers) some way in which a computer helps with a job (some way not mentioned in this reading).

2. Talk with someone who works with a computer about its benefits and problems.

3. List the similarities and the differences between using a typewriter and a computer.

4. Read twenty job descriptions in a newspaper employment section. What percentage of the jobs require experience with computers? Compare your results with those of other students.

Topics for Further Discussion or Writing

1. Some experts think that computers will make office work obsolete, and that many people will be able to work at home. How would that affect our life styles?

2. How important will computers be in the work that you plan to do? What tasks can computers perform in this work?

3. How will computers make work less pleasant for human beings?

4. Describe an experience in which computer use in an office or other workplace has affected you.

———————————

A Last Chance for Computers in the Schools?

Before You Read

Peter H. Wagschal, dean of program planning and development at the School of Education, University of Massachusetts-Amherst, wrote this article for the *Phi Delta Kappan* magazine. He sees some interesting similarities between the effect of computers in schools today and the effect of television thirty years ago.

Think About It

Was TV used often in your elementary or high school?

To what extent are computers being used in your country's schools?

A Last Chance for Computers in the Schools?

Peter H. Wagschal

1 For the first time, the major manufacturers of computers are beginning to think seriously about the schools as a potential market for their products. The problem for these manufacturers, of course, is that U.S. education has shown remarkable resistance in the past to invasion by new technologies. And, although the public is treated almost daily to reports in the media on the extensive and growing use of computers in U.S. schools, the reality behind those statistics is less than encouraging to those of us who see an important place for computers in education.

2 For example, my own local school system has invested what it considers to be a substantial (even painful, in these lean times) sum of money in computers for its elementary schools. Yet my son, who attends an elementary school in that system, currently finds himself in the less-than-privileged position of being able to spend approximately 30 minutes every two weeks playing educational games on a three-year-old Apple.

3 In my talks with public school teachers and administrators about the potential impact of computers on their daily operations, I have been struck by the overwhelming similarities between what the schools are doing and thinking about microcomputers these days and what they did and thought about television some three decades ago. . . .

4 In 1947 there were approximately 7,000 television sets in the U.S. Seven years later, roughly 80% of all American households had at least one television set, and by 1980 there were more television sets in America than bathtubs — a fact that led some observers to ask which we wash more often, our bodies or our brains.

5 During the past three decades the average American has watched four to six hours of television programming every day. By the time U.S. youngsters graduate from high school, they have spent more time watching television than in any other activity except sleeping.

6   In the early years of television, school officials believed that this medium had the potential to revolutionize classroom instruction. During the late 1950s and early 1960s, many — perhaps most — U.S. schools purchased television sets, intending to use them to radically improve the quality of education.

7   My own local school system still has the remnants of those purchases. And, once again, the experiences of my own children with television in school are fairly typical. The broadcasting studios in my children's school are seldom used and in a severe state of disrepair. The television sets that still work are brought into the classrooms only on very special occasions, most notably when the space shuttle goes into orbit or sets down again. Meanwhile, of course, my children — and children across the U.S. — are spending the majority of their out-of-school hours glued to the tube. Yet their typical school day proceeds as if television did not exist.

8   There are at least three explanations for the failure of television to capture the interest and imagination of public school educators, and these explanations will prove instructive for educators who are now coming to grips with the computer revolution. First, the schools that purchased television sets rarely had the foresight to set aside money for equipment repairs and maintenance. Second, these schools never found an effective way to train teachers to integrate television into their ongoing instructional programs. Third, and perhaps most important, a majority of teachers had (and still have) an extremely snobbish attitude regarding the quality of commercial television and its consequent usefulness in the classroom.

9   There is irony here. Although the content of commercial television fails in general to meet the high standards of public school teachers, it nonetheless consumes most of the free time of the students they teach. And the ideas, values, and attitudes purveyed by "Dallas," "The A-Team," "Webster," and similar programs are passed to these youngsters undiluted by any form of critical thinking — precisely *because* the schools have been unable or unwilling to grant a place to commercial television in the classroom.

10   A considerable body of research suggests that the content of commercial television shapes viewers' notions of reality. For example, a survey conducted in a small midwestern town in 1979 asked residents to name the most serious problem facing their community. The overwhelming response was "crime in the streets," even though no serious crime had taken place in the town for more than two decades. Meanwhile, another research study in the late 1970s investigated police procedures in Los Angeles; the researchers discovered that the day-to-day operations of the Los Angeles police force mimicked the procedures followed in the most popular crime shows on television.

11   Such findings should not come as a surprise. Most of us have never been arrested, for example, yet we all feel that we know what that process is like, having observed it so often on television. Like it or not, the enormous amount of time we spend watching television has invested the images we see on the screen with a degree of reality that often causes us to discount our own experiences, when they fail to match that on-screen reality.

12   The public schools work hard for 12 years to turn our children into critical readers, even though recent statistics show that adults in the U.S. read an average of one book each per year. At the same time, the public schools have abdicated responsibility for helping children deal critically with television, even though these students are (and will be) watching four to six hours of television programming every day of their lives.

13   Today, some 30 years after the emergence of television as a national pastime, we can perceive the beginnings of another technological revolution whose pace is certainly no slower and whose impact is certainly no less extensive than that of television. The major question in this nation is no longer *whether* home computers will saturate the U.S. market, but *when* and *in what form?*

14   As home computers become less costly and more "user friendly," we will find it increasingly difficult to resist them. In the not-too-distant future, virtually every American will be spending roughly the same amount of time actively interacting with some kind of computer as we now spend passively staring at our television sets. The question that troubles me is, What are the schools going to be doing with computers when that not-too-distant future arrives?

Comprehension

1. Which of the statements below best describes the author's point in paragraphs 1 and 2?

    a. Computers have already assumed an important place in U.S. schools.
    b. U.S. schools have been very slow to use new technologies in education.
    c. U.S. schools have been very quick to use new technologies in education.

2. To what extent is television being used in U.S. education?

3. Wagschal thinks that television has not attracted U.S. educators because

    a. the equipment and maintenance are too expensive.
    b. educators think that students are watching too much TV.
    c. teachers don't think that commercial television is very good.

4. Irony means using words that express something opposite to the meaning of a thought in order to emphasize that thought. For example: The irony is that the efficiency expert talked for four hours about how we could do our work faster. What is the irony mentioned in paragraph 9 of the reading?

5. What are some of the effects of commercial TV on schoolchildren?

Discussion

1. If educators react to computers as they reacted to TV, they will not use computers extensively in schools. Why would they not use them?

2. Are there other technical innovations that are not being used because of difficulties similar to those described by Wagschal? In education? In industry? In agriculture?

3. Do you think the schools are responsible for teaching children how to watch commercial TV? Why?

Match the terms in Column A with the correct definitions or explanations in Column B by writing the appropriate number in the blanks.

A	B
1. less than encouraging	_____ what is left
2. struck	_____ approximately
3. discount	_____ almost
4. abdicate	_____ a period of ten years
5. roughly	_____ fill completely
6. saturate	_____ without a great deal of hope
7. decade	_____ give less value to
8. virtually	_____ strongly affected
9. remnants	_____ give up responsibility

Choose five words or phrases from Column A above and write a sentence using each one.

1. _____

2. _____

3. _____

4. _____

5. _____

Fill in the blanks in the sentences below with words from this list:

potential	invasion	seldom	fairly
substantial	reality	rarely	extremely
typical	impact	daily	less
late	foresight		more
major			

1. The development of computers has not had a _____ effect on how children are being educated today.

2. The _____ social _____ of computers on the workplace has led bosses to arrange schedules so that the workers will not spend too much time alone at their machines.

3. In 1980 there were _____ bathtubs than television sets in the United States.

4. On a _____ evening, U.S. children may watch two or three hours of television; however, if the children have to go to school the next day, their parents will probably not let them watch the _____ evening programs.

5. Children _____ use computers for help in their _____ classes.

6. The author suggests that the way we look at _____ is influenced by what we see on television.

7. Manufacturers of computers are _____ interested in having educators learn how to use the new machines.

8. In some countries adults read a _____ number of books each year, but in the United States they read an average of one book per year.

9. U.S. children spend _____ time watching television than sleeping.

10. If we had enough _____ , we would know how U.S. education will use computers.

It is clear that the computer has great potential benefits for education. In two or three sentences, describe another invention or plan that has great potential benefits for some aspect of society.

_____

_____

_____

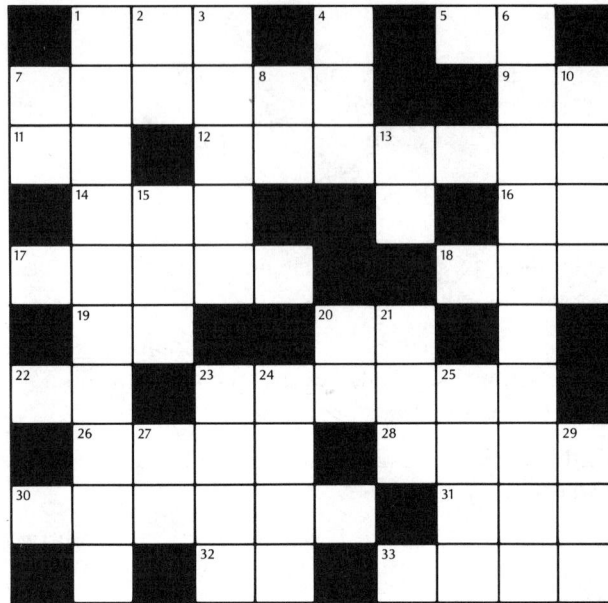

(For answers, see page 54.)

Across

1. Boy's nickname *OR* Comes before . . . vation, . . . ute, . . . utation, . . . vage

5. Comes before A.D.

7. Go to (school, for example)

9. All right

11. Degree after B.A.

12. Hobby

14. Something to wear around the neck

16. Possessive adjective

17. Suffix for "small"

18. Affirmative reply

19. Abbreviation for southeast

20. Musical note

22. 12 inches (abbreviation)

23. Open to all (library, for example)

26. Colored part of the eye

28. Prepare something for publication

30. Where you see the image on a computer

31. Auditory receiver

32. Older than a Jr.

33. Abstract "watch" artist

Down

1. Mathematical data
2. Preposition related to time
3. Person with a skin disease
4. Items that try to sell goods
6. TV visual to sell goods
7. Morning time
8. Continent abbreviation
10. Needed to enter data into a computer
13. Where you see number 6 down

15. Hard, cold water
20. 16 ounces (abbreviation)
21. Beer's cousin
23. Tart's cousins
24. Some are "——— friendly"
25. Thought
27. Train station abbreviation
29. Suffix for "three"

The author writes that U.S. education has resisted new technologies. On the lines below, give a brief example of resistance to a new technology or idea in your country.

_____

_____

The author writes that television affects the way we look at reality and gives two examples to support his point. Retell his examples in your own words on the lines below.

_____

_____

_____

_____

_____

_____

Complete this paragraph by inserting appropriate words in the blanks.

So far, teachers' attitudes _____ computers in schools have some

striking parallels with their previous _____ toward television. In my

visits to schools, for example, I hear teachers complaining about the dehuman-

izing _____ of computers on their users. They also talk about the ____

_____ danger that could come if computers were _____ to es-

tablish a central control in the nation. But whether we like computers or

_____ , these machines are going to play a _____ role in our

_____ lives. The discomfort of educators with computers will not stop

the _____ of this new electronic technology into our lives.

Follow-up Activities

1. Survey your classmates to find out how many books they read in a year. Also find out when and what kinds of books they read.

2. Survey your classmates about TV usage in their schools. Ask for what purposes and how often TV was used.

3. Look for a magazine or newspaper article on computers or talk with somebody who works with a computer. Identify some advantages and disadvantages of computers and be prepared to describe them to the class.

4. Is there an educational use for computers in your academic field? Describe it.

The Computer Fallacy

Before You Read

Joseph Weizenbaum, a professor of computer science at the Massachusetts Institute of Technology, is a pioneer in the development of the computer: he invented the famous Eliza computer program, making it possible for a computer to converse with humans. In this interview with Franz-Olivier Giesbert of *Le Nouvel Observateur*, Weizenbaum offers a dissenting view on what he calls the computer fad.

Think About It

What are "fads"?

How do you think television has affected creativity in children?

What is a fallacy?

The Computer Fallacy

Franz-Olivier Giesbert

1 NOUVEL OBSERVATEUR: Computers are arriving everywhere — in offices, in schools, in the home. Shouldn't this delight you?

2 JOSEPH WEIZENBAUM: I am not a computer salesman. All I can hope is that the technology I helped to develop be used well. But it isn't — far from it.

3 NOUVEL OBSERVATEUR: What do you have in mind?

4 WEIZENBAUM: The fad for home and school computers that is creating such a furor in the United States, as well as in Great Britain and France, for example. A new human malady has been invented, just as the makers of patent medicines in the past invented illnesses such as "tired blood" in order to create a market for their products. Now it's computer illiteracy. The future, we are told, will belong to those familiar with the computer. What a joke this would be if only it didn't victimize so many innocent bystanders. It reminds me of the old encyclopedia fad: "If you buy one," proclaimed the salesmen, "your child will do better in school and succeed in life." And parents complied. But the encyclopedia was rarely consulted and was soon retired to the shelves.

5 The infatuation with television, that other "educational" instrument, also comes to mind. Thanks to TV, kids didn't make as much noise as before. And from that people concluded that TV taught them good behavior.

6 NOUVEL OBSERVATEUR: But you wouldn't compare television, which renders the viewer passive, with the computer, which develops creativity?

7 WEIZENBAUM: Why not? With television, a kid will watch a fighter pilot shoot down a plane piloted by another human being. With video games, the child "becomes" the fighter pilot. The difference? In both cases, the child inhabits an abstract world in which actions have no consequences, in which violence is truly mindless. Video games are, if anything, more harmful than TV, because they *actively* teach dissociation between what one does and the consequences of one's actions.

8   As for the computer itself, I think it inhibits children's creativity. In most cases, the computer programs kids and not the other way around. Once they have started a program, the computer may leave them a few degrees of freedom, to be sure, but on the whole it will tell them what to do and when to do it. My colleague Seymour Papert claims that he has a radically different approach: with his system, he says, the children program the computer. He made a film that was supposed to illustrate his thesis. In it one sees children working on Logo [Papert's educational computer system] in Senegal, Scotland, and Texas. As if by chance, they all drew exactly the same picture on their computers: a flower made out of ellipsoids strung together. Strange, isn't it?

9   NOUVEL OBSERVATEUR: Even so, don't you think that the use of computers reinforces a child's problem-solving ability?

10   WEIZENBAUM: If that were true, then computer professionals would lead better lives than the rest of the population. We know very well that that isn't the case.

11   There is, as far as I know, no more evidence that programming is good for the mind than Latin is, as is sometimes claimed.

12   NOUVEL OBSERVATEUR: Would you deny that the computer revolution will affect social equality?

13   WEIZENBAUM: Graduates of the Massachusetts Institute of Technology are required to pass a swimming exam. Assuming that MIT graduates are disproportionately represented among the leaders of the American high-technology industry, a simple-minded statistician would wrongly infer a cause-and-effect relationship between the ability to swim and managerial success. There's a risk that the same thing will happen with computers. Right now, the children of the well-to-do are given liberal access to computers. People may very well attribute the success of these children to their computer experience. In reality, these children will have had many other important advantages right from the start. If you want to reduce inequality, the solution is to give the poor money, not computers.

14   NOUVEL OBSERVATEUR: Do you think, then, that France is making a mistake by trying to put computers in everyone's hands?

15   WEIZENBAUM: If that is what France is doing, then, yes, it's making a mistake. The temptation to send in computers wherever there is a problem is great. There's hunger in the Third World. So computerize. The schools are in trouble. So bring in computers. The introduction of the computer into any problem area, be it medicine, education, or whatever, usually creates the impression that grievous deficiencies are being corrected, that something is being done. But often its principal effect is to push problems even further into obscurity — to avoid confrontation with the need for fundamentally critical thinking.

Comprehension

1. Why does the *Nouvel Observateur* interviewer expect that Weizenbaum will be happy with the idea that "computers are arriving everywhere?"

2. To what does Weizenbaum compare "computer illiteracy?"

3. According to Weizenbaum, what do TV and video games have in common? Why does he think video games are worse?

4. Does Weizenbaum think that the computer stimulates children's creativity? What evidence does he give to support his view? What do you think of this evidence?

5. What point does Weizenbaum make with the swimming exam example?

6. Does Weizenbaum think that making computers available to everybody, including the very poor, would help reduce social inequality?

Discussion

1. Do you think that making computers available to everybody would help reduce social inequality?

2. Do you think the study of Latin or another ancient language is good for the mind? Why or why not?

3. What do you think *critical thinking* means? What is Weizenbaum's attitude toward it?

4. Why do you think there is so much violence in entertainment (TV, movies, video games, sports)?

Language Practice

If you think a statement below is true, put a T in the blank next to it. If you think a statement is false, put an F.

1. _____ Weizenbaum is a computer salesman.

2. _____ The Eliza computer program allows one computer to talk to another computer.

3. _____ Weizenbaum believes that people do not use encyclopedias very much.

4. _____ Weizenbaum thinks that children learn good behavior from TV.

5. _____ The *Nouvel Observateur* reporter believes that although people watching TV are passive, those working with a computer are active.

6. _____ The children working on Logo in Senegal drew very different pictures from those in Texas.

7. _____ Weizenbaum believes that computer professionals lead better lives than the rest of the population.

8. _____ Weizenbaum thinks that introducing computers into education and medicine only creates an impression that something is being done to solve a problem.

9. _____ Weizenbaum says that the success of well-to-do children results from their experience with computers.

After you correct the true or false exercise above, reread the false statements. Correct the false statements by writing the correct information on the lines below.

EXAMPLE: _____ "The Computer Fallacy" is about the mechanical problems of computers.

"The Computer Fallacy" is not about mechanical problems. It is about the uses and the effects of the uses of computers.

_____

_____

_____

_____

_____

_____

_____

The following are definitions of words in the reading. Find the appropriate word, then write it in the blank.

1. sickness (See paragraph 4.)   _____

2. an interest or activity that does not last very long (See paragraph 5.)   _____

3. make someone be a victim (See paragraph 4.)   _____

4. do what has been asked or ordered (See paragraph 4.)   _____

5. without a connection (See paragraph 7.)   _____

6. darkness (See paragraph 15.)   _____

7. results (noun) (See paragraph 7.)   _____

8. a person who is near an event but who is not part of it (See paragraph 4.)   _____

9. holds back (See paragraph 8.)   _____

10. get a meaning from something (See paragraph 13.)   _____

The sentence "The bystander was hurt" reports a result (or an effect). On the lines below, write a sentence that describes a possible cause for that effect.

_____

_____

Hunger can be a cause. Write a sentence that describes one possible effect of hunger.

_____

_____

Actions often have consequences. On the lines below, briefly describe an action that had an expected consequence.

_____

_____

_____

Weizenbaum describes home computers as a fad. In two or three sentences, describe a recent fad in your country.

_____

_____

_____

_____

Choose the appropriate forms of the words in each set below and write them in the blanks.

1. infatuate   infatuated   infatuation

   Many people are _____ with video games. Some sociologists think that the games _____ people because they demand total attention. Others think that the _____ is a consequence of the identification of the player with the machine.

2. tempt   tempting   temptation

   It is clear that video games are a _____ for some children, especially adolescents. What may _____ them is the feeling of control that they have when they play the games. For adolescents who want to escape from their problems, the world of video games is _____ .

3. conclude   conclusive   conclusion

   Since the interviewer from the *Nouvel Observateur* thinks that computers encourage thinking and creative activity among children, he'll probably _____ that computers are important for education. But Weizenbaum wouldn't agree with that _____ . He might ask us to see how schools use computers before we say that the evidence for computers' benefits to education is _____ .

Follow-up Activities

1. Find out how your classmates (or friends) respond to video games. How many play them? How often do they play? Why do they like or not like them?

2. Do men and women have the same attitudes toward computers? Ask equal numbers of men and women this question: If you had a computer and some free time, what would you use it for? Compare the answers of the men and the women.

3. Some communities will not allow stores full of video games within their boundaries; some communities will not allow the showing of certain movies. Look up the subject of censorship and read about one incident; find out what the problem was and what happened.

4. Ask two professionals, one in the humanities and one in science, this question: Do you think computers have great potential for education? Compare their answers with this comment by Sherry Turkle (*People*, May 31, 1982):

> You get kids playing with computers who never before thought they could handle anything scientific or mathematical. And the technically minded kids often have their first experience creating something other people find beautiful.

Chapter Review

1. Review the selections in this chapter and list positive and negative aspects of the computer.

2. Compare the readings and find two points of agreement between any two authors.

3. Someone said that computers may be able to think but they can't dream. How would you interpret this?

4. Researchers discovered that the Los Angeles police imitated procedures they saw on popular TV crime shows. What are some other indications that people imitate what they see on TV?

5. A ten-year-old girl doesn't want to go to computer camp. Her mother worries that if the girl doesn't learn about computers, she won't be able to get a job in the future. Her father says that it is more important for her to learn math, to learn to ask intelligent questions, and to be able to understand data. What do you think? How important is computer training? At what level of schooling should it take place?

Answers to crossword puzzle.

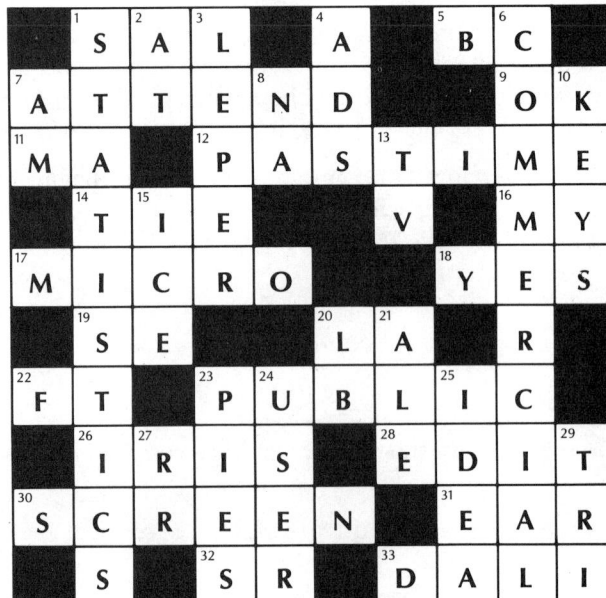

		1 S	2 A	3 L		4 A		5 B	6 C	
7 A	T	T	E	8 N	D			9 O	10 K	
11 M	A		12 P	A	S	13 T	I	M	E	
	14 T	15 I	E			V		16 M	Y	
17 M	I	C	R	O			18 Y	E	S	
	19 S	E			20 L	21 A		R		
22 F	T		23 P	24 U	B	L	25 I	C		
	26 I	27 R	I	S		28 E	D	I	29 T	
30 S	C	R	E	E	N		31 E	A	R	
	S		32 S	R		33 D	A	L	I	

Looking at the Law

3

All societies have laws, and contemporary societies seem to have too many laws. But as a result of new social relationships and a technology that can keep people alive for a long time, there are many new questions that must be decided by law. In this chapter two lawyers discuss some of these questions and some of the answers provided by the law courts.

When Eating Out Is Against the Law

Before You Read

Neil Chayet, a lawyer, discusses interesting aspects of the law on the radio program "Looking at the Law." In this reading, Chayet tells us about a surprising regulation.

Think About It

Are there any laws or regulations in your country or elsewhere that seem surprising to you?

Do people employ lawyers frequently in your country? For what kinds of problems?

When Eating Out Is Against the Law

Neil Chayet

1 Is it against the law to eat at the airport? Lest you think this question is ridiculous, let me tell you what happened to me recently at Boston's Logan International. I arrived at the airport and asked the agent if the 1:00 P.M. flight I was headed for was a lunch flight. He answered that no food at all was served on the flight. I had eaten at 6:00 in the morning and decided that I would go to the cafeteria at the airport and get a sandwich to take on the plane.

2 I ordered a hamburger and then asked the short-order cook to wrap it. He looked at me as if I had just suggested he join me in an international smuggling ring. He explained that no food could be taken out of the restaurant and that if he put the hamburger on anything but a plate, he would be in big trouble.

3 So I took the hamburger on a plate, paid $1.50 for it, then took it off the plate and started to wrap it up in napkins. As I was doing this, a young woman obviously in authority approached me and asked what I was doing. I replied that I was wrapping my hamburger up in a napkin. She said that I could not take it out of the restaurant. I said that I had only ten minutes until my plane took off; and she said that that was plenty of time for me to sit down and eat my hamburger. I said, "I am walking out of here with my hamburger." She said, "You can't." I asked why, and then she said it: "It's against the law." Now, I haven't read all the FAA regulations, but I found it difficult to believe that there was a law forbidding me to eat a hamburger on the plane. I know you can't take your own alcoholic beverages to drink on the plane, but this was only a hamburger.

4 I decided to chance it. I slowly backed away from her, holding my hamburger, and headed for the gate, hoping my hamburger, which by this time had become rather cold and heavy, wouldn't set off the metal detector. As I ate it on the plane during takeoff, I wondered if it had all been worth it.

5 When I got back to Boston, I called the port authority and was referred to a helpful gentleman who informed me that the reason for my difficulties was that if people could take food out of the restaurant, they would mess up the new carpets that had been recently installed. It was related, he said, to the reason you can't buy gum in the terminal, even though you might like to have it for when your ears get blocked up. Thanks to his efforts, though, the policy on food at least has changed. Although you are not encouraged to take food out, it *will* be wrapped up for you if you request it, and you *can* take it with you — without breaking the law.

Comprehension

Expand your understanding of the reading's main ideas.

1. Why did Chayet want to buy a hamburger at the airport?

2. Why didn't the cook wrap the hamburger for Chayet to take out?

3. What did Chayet mean when he said that the hamburger had become cold and heavy and that he hoped it wouldn't set off the metal detector?

4. What reason was Chayet given for people not being permitted to take food out of the airport restaurant?

5. What else can't you buy at this airport? Why would you want to buy this item at an airport?

Applications

Relate the reading to events in your own life.

1. What are some other regulations that airports, bus terminals, or train stations have for passengers and visitors? What are the reasons for those regulations?

2. What are some regulations or laws that seem ridiculous to you? Why?

3. Chayet found it difficult to believe that he couldn't take a hamburger out of the restaurant. Describe some similar things that you find difficult to believe. Write sentences that begin, "I find/found it difficult to believe that . . . ."

4. What are some laws or regulations that you feel are necessary for: a classroom, a subway, a dormitory, a cafeteria? Give reasons.

The Best Interests of the Child
and
After Divorce, Where Do All the Children Go?

Before You Read

These selections, also by Neil Chayet, concern some human and legal difficulties that occur when people divorce.

Think About It

Do you know children whose parents were divorced? How have the children adjusted to their situation?

Is divorce common in your country? If it is, how often do legal problems occur?

The Best Interests of the Child

Neil Chayet

1   By far the most serious and tragic side of divorce is the pain and trauma that is visited on the children. Often the most bitter cases found anywhere in the system by which we resolve disputes are found where one parent battles the other for the custody of their children. . . . The factor that makes them all virtually the same is the harm that they do to the parents and children involved.

2   The standard most often quoted is, "What's in the best interests of the child?" The only problem is that *both* parties claim to know exactly what is in the best interests of their children. Sometimes one parent is right, sometimes the other, and, tragically, sometimes neither. It often seems that everyone has a different theory. Some say that the children's relationship with both parents should continue; some say that there should be finality and that the relationship with the parent with whom the child does not live should be minimized. Some say that there should be a lawyer for the husband, a lawyer for the wife, and a lawyer for the child — leaving unresolved for the moment how these lawyers are to be selected or paid.

3   Some stress leaving some of the decisions to the children themselves. The difficulty with this approach was pointed out by a recent New York case in which two of the children, custody of whom had been given to the mother, decided they wanted to live with their father, one of their reasons being that he had a nicer house. The court denied the change, stating that the best interests of the child, particularly over the long term, often require the overbalancing of subjective desires by more dependable objective criteria. But perhaps the most meaningful language of all is found in the same case, where it was stated, "Most crucial is a gentle, wise, and forebearing attitude on the part of the parents, when a mother and father continue to be devoted to their youngsters."

4   In recent years, many divorcing couples have sought to avoid this trauma, with custody resting in one parent and reasonable visitation in the other, or even with the developing concept of joint custody. Most important, many people are hoping that some day the disciplines of law, psychiatry, psychology, and sociology will be able to tell us what *really* is in the best interests of the child.

After Divorce, Where Do All the Children Go?

Neil Chayet

1   After a divorce, how much choice should a child have in deciding where to live? That was the question decided by the Court of Appeals for the state of Oregon. A couple was divorced a number of years back and the wife received custody of two daughters aged five and three. A few years after the divorce, the mother's emotional and physical health began to deteriorate, and she voluntarily turned her children over to her former husband, who by this time had remarried and had two more children by his second wife.

2   Two years later, after the mother had fully recovered, she asked that the daughters be returned. When her husband refused, she went to court seeking to have custody of the children, who were now nine and eleven, restored.

3   The court family counselor recommended that the children stay with their father, and the doctor who'd taken care of them since birth recommended the same thing. In addition, the children's school-teacher joined in the recommendation, saying that the girls got along very well with their stepmother and were doing very well in their school work. The only problem was that the father was getting ready to move to Seattle, and the children would have to leave Portland and go with him.

4   At this point the judges decided to interview the girls themselves in their chambers. The older daughter said she would rather stay in Portland with her mother than move to Seattle with her father. The younger child said it wasn't that she loved one of her parents more than the other, but she would rather not move to a new community, and she added, "In a way, I should live with my mother because she is my real mother."

5   After hearing from the children, the judges decided a material change in circumstances had occurred, since the mother was now physically and mentally recovered, and they had the right to order a change in custody if they wanted to. And because the daughters said they wanted to go with their mother, the court decided to let that fact override all of the other opinions. The court said in determining what's in the best interest of the children, we must give weight to the girls' preferences, and the court joined the growing trend around the nation to allow children to decide with which parent they want to live. One judge dissented, saying that the wishes of the children should not override all of the other opinions, but the majority ruled. When it comes to deciding where to live, children do have a choice after all.

Comprehension

1. What do you feel to be the saddest, most difficult aspect of divorce for a family? Why?

2. What do some people believe should happen "in the best interests of the children" when a couple divorces?

3. After a divorce, do the courts allow children to decide where they want to live? Support your answer with an example from the reading.

4. Why did the divorced woman from Portland, Oregon, give her former husband custody of their two daughters?

5. When the Portland mother wanted the girls returned to her, who recommended that the children stay with their father? Why?

6. What was the one major problem in this case? What did the judges finally decide to do about it?

7. What did the two girls tell the judges?

8. What finally happened in this case?

Discussion

1. What are some major problems that could lead to divorce?

2. Do you think divorce should be easily available? Why? Why not?

3. What part should children play in a divorce action?

Language Practice

Substitute a word or phrase from the following list for an underlined word or phrase in the sentences below and rewrite the sentences.

disagreed	hurt	the divorced parents
get worse	strongly suggested	saddest

1. Both parties say they know what is best for the children. _____

   _____

2. The court decided to let the mother have custody; one judge dissented.

   _____

3. The court family counselor <u>recommended</u> that the children stay with their

father. _____

_____

4. The mother's emotional and physical health began to <u>deteriorate</u>.

_____

_____

5. The <u>most tragic</u> side of divorce is the <u>pain</u> that the children experience.

_____

_____

Choose the appropriate forms of the words in each set below and write them in the blanks.

1. resolution   unresolved   resolve

When a married couple is unable to _____ their differences, they usually end their marriage. They feel getting divorced is the only _____ , especially if they have been getting counseling help for some time. Leaving their _____ marital problems behind them, they go into the future looking for something they thought they had once found in their marriage.

2. recommendation   recommend

In divorce cases, lawyers often _____ that children stay with their mother. The judge will listen to the lawyer's _____ , but ultimately the judge will make the final decision based on the best interests of the children.

3.   wisdom   wise   wisely

_____ parents will never think only of their own needs in a divorce.

A caring parent will consider all the alternatives _____ before making

a final decision, even if it means losing custody of the children. The _____

_____ of the parents' decision usually makes it easier for the children

to adjust to the trauma of the divorce.

4.   preference   prefer   preferable   preferably

In the past, the courts usually found it _____ for children to live

with their mother. Today, however, many courts _____ to allow the

children to make this decision. _____ it is in the children's best interest

to take part in the decision-making process. Asking for a child's _____

can make the divorce less painful.

For each of the following verbs, write its definition, and then write sentences using it and answering the questions, as in the example below.

recover   volunteer   restore   deny

EXAMPLE: flee

Definition: _to run away_
                   to escape

Who? What?   _People who are in trouble flee._
                   Animals flee from danger.

Where?   _Animals flee to a safe place._
                   Refugees flee from one country to
                   another. Criminals flee from prison.

When?

Why?

*Children flee when they're afraid
Some criminals flee at night.
Some people flee because they're not
happy. In the 1920s, immigrants fled
Europe to find a better place to live.*

WORD: restore

Definition: _____

Who? What? _____

_____

Where? _____

_____

When? _____

_____

Why? _____

_____

Do the other words on another piece of paper.

Fill in the blanks in the paragraph below with words from this list:

custody   divorcing   former   joint custody   visitation

When a couple divorces, it is not unusual for the wife to receive _____

_____ of their children. The children's father usually has _____

rights; that is, he has the right to see his children on weekends, holidays, and

school and summer vacations. In recent years, many _____ couples

have chosen to have _____ , where the _____ spouses (hus-

bands or wives) divide the time spent with the children equally between mother

and father.

Combine the sentences below by following the directions for each set. Try to eliminate as many words as possible without changing the main ideas. Use pronouns where appropriate. Do not use a dictionary.

EXAMPLE: She went to court seeking custody of the children. They were nine and eleven. (Use *who*.)

She went to court seeking custody of the children who were now nine and eleven.

1. The mother claims to know what is in the best interest of their children. So does the father. (Use *both*.)

    _____

2. She voluntarily turned her children over to her former husband. He had remarried by this time. (Use *who*.)

    _____

3. The children wanted to stay with their father. They would have to leave their hometown. They would have to go with him. (Use *if*; eliminate words and use *and*.)

    _____

4. I should live with my mother. She is my real mother. (Use *because*.)

    _____

Complete the following sentences by using an appropriate "question word" such as *who*, *where*, or *when* and an infinitive.

EXAMPLE: When you have to make a decision, you sometimes don't know

    what to do   .

1. When a couple has marital problems, they sometimes don't know _____

    _____ for help.

2. When a couple decides to get a divorce, they aren't sure _____

    _____ their children about it.

3. The court usually tells the husband _____

to the wife for child support.

4. Some parents don't know _____ their children adjust to a divorce.

5. Some children are confused after a divorce and can't decide _____

_____ .

When you first leave home to live on your own, you must make decisions, learn some new skills, and find out about certain things. On the lines below, write about some of your decisions, and some skills and information you needed.

1. I had to decide where to live.

2. I had to decide how much rent I could afford.

3. _____

4. _____

5. _____

6. _____

7. _____

We have to make decisions every day. Make decisions about the following choices. On the lines below, write your own sentences using *would rather (not)* . . . *because* . . .

EXAMPLE: I *would rather* study business than law *because* I could help my father in his company when I graduate.

Here are some decisions:
To marry when young or when old
To have or not have children
To have a profession or to raise a family
To get married or to remain single

Add one of your own choices to the list above and write your decision about it on line 5.

1. _____

2. _____

3. _____

4. _____

5. _____

Follow-up Activities

1. Using the choices from the previous exercise, compare your decisions with those made by friends or classmates on the same subjects. Prepare a summary of the results.

2. Many books, magazines, TV programs, and movies deal with love, marriage, and divorce. Choose one that you have read or seen recently and be prepared to report on it for the class.

3. In many newspapers there is a column that helps people who write asking for advice on their problems. Find one column that discusses a problem about marriage or divorce and bring it into class. Prepare a letter that you would write as a response to the problem. You might read the problem to others in the class and find out how they would respond.

4. Describe the judge's decision in the Oregon case to three or four people and find out if they agree or disagree with it.

Topics for Further Discussion or Writing

1. Besides divorce, what are some ways in which people (in various countries) solve their marital problems?

2. What legal rights should children have in divorce cases?

3. Why is divorce not legal in some countries?

4. Is the law profession an attractive career in your country? Why or why not?

What's in a Name?
and
Can You Change Your Name?

Before You Read

In these readings, Neil Chayet discusses a topic relevant to many people nowadays as they travel from country to country and encounter different ways of using names.

Think About It

Have you had any problems with your name? Is it easy or hard for other people to pronounce or spell?

Do you know any people who have changed their names? Why?

What's in a Name?

Neil Chayet

1   William Shakespeare once asked the question, "What's in a name?" According to a recent opinion of the Maryland attorney general, the answer is, "Not much." The opinion was issued recently as a result of a question from the state registrar of vital records. The question was whether or not the registrar could legally require that the last name of a newborn child placed on a birth certificate be the same as one of its parents'.

2   The Maryland attorney general noted that this question is on people's minds all over the country. With women no longer automatically taking on the last name of their husband, and with people living together unmarried, it was predictable that a father's last name, a mother's last name, a hyphenated name, or a completely new name would be placed on a birth certificate, to the dismay of the keepers of the records. The recordkeepers are worried as to how future generations will ever find their roots if the names are not the same.

3   The attorney general reviewed recent cases in the area. In one, a woman who remarried wanted to change the last names of her children by her first marriage because she claimed the children were being teased at school because their last names weren't the same as hers. The natural father protested, and the court refused to allow the change of name in the long-term best interest of the children. Also reviewed was a recent case decided by the Supreme Judicial Court of Massa-

chusetts holding that town clerks simply did not have authority to tell people what their names could or could not be. That court added that freedom of personal choice in family life is one of the liberties protected by the due process clause of the Fourteenth Amendment, and there is a private realm of family life that the state cannot enter. As for administrative confusion, the Maryland attorney general noted that that can be solved by cross-indexing.

4   As for the question, "What's in a name?" Shakespeare's answer may still be the best: "That which we call a rose by any other name would smell as sweet."

Can You Change Your Name?

Neil Chayet

5   Can you change your name just because you feel like it? Well, at the moment, the answer appears to be yes in Virginia and no in New York. The Virginia case involved two women who wanted to take their maiden names back, even though they were still married. The lower court in Virginia denied the petitions for change of name on the ground that Virginia law, like that of many states, allowed a married woman to resume her maiden name *after* she was divorced. But the Virginia Supreme Court reversed the lower court, saying that there was nothing in the law that indicated that a name could *only* be changed after divorce.

6   The court then pointed out that under the common law, a person is free to adopt any name as long as it's not for a fraudulent purpose or to cheat creditors.

7   If you live in New York, however, you may well have a more difficult time changing your name. A woman named Cooperman went to court to have her named changed to Cooperperson. She went to court, she said, because she believed in the feminist cause and because she felt that the name Cooperperson "more properly reflects her sense of human equality than does the name Cooperman." But New York Supreme Court Justice John Scileppi did not agree with Miss Cooperman's reasoning and refused to grant the change-of-name request. The judge gave a number of examples of what could happen if he granted the request, stating that he would next encounter someone named Jackson trying to change that name to Jackchild, or Manning wanting to be known as Peopleing, or a woman named Carmen wanting to be called Carperson. Judge Scileppi wrote that "the possibilities are virtually endless and increasingly inane, and this would truly be in the realm of nonsense." So Miss Cooperman will remain Miss Cooperman, unless she gets married . . . or moves to Virginia.

Comprehension

What's in a Name?

1. What are recordkeepers worried about?

2. What reasons are given in the story for last-name changes?

3. Why can't local government tell people what their names can and can't be?

4. What solution to this problem of "many names" is mentioned in the reading?

Can You Change Your Name?

1. According to the reading, what is the legal decision about a woman who wants to change from her married name to her maiden name?

2. What do the Virginia courts say about a person who wants to adopt any name?

3. Why did the New York woman want to change her name?

4. What did the judge finally decide to do about this case? Why?

Rewrite the following sentences on the lines below, substituting your own words for the underlined words. The new sentences should express the same idea as the original sentences.

1. The recordkeepers are worried <u>as to how future generations will ever find their roots</u> if the names are not the same. (See paragraph 2.)

_____

_____

2. A woman who remarried wanted to change the last names of her children by her first marriage; the <u>natural</u> father <u>protested</u>. (See paragraph 3.)

_____

3. Can you change your name just because you <u>feel like it</u>? (See paragraph 5.)

_____

4. Two women wanted to <u>take their maiden names back</u>. (See paragraph 5.)

_____

5. A woman who remarried wanted to change the last names of her children
    by her first marriage because she claimed <u>the children were being teased at
    school</u> because their last names weren't the same as hers. (See paragraph
    3.)

    _____

    _____

6. The Maryland attorney general noted that <u>this question is on people's
    minds all over the country</u>. (See paragraph 2.)

    _____

Read the following definitions. Then for each one, fill in the blank with an
appropriate word from the reading.

1. A person who has legal authority to help others when
    they are in trouble with the law (See paragraph 1.)   _____

2. Specific information that is written and kept for future
    reference (See paragraph 2.)   _____

3. A person whose duty is to keep records for a town or a
    university (See paragraph 1 or paragraph 2.)   _____

4. A written statement made by someone in authority which
    can be used as proof or evidence of something (See par-
    agraph 1.)   _____

5. An average period of time during which children grow
    up, marry, and have children of their own (See paragraph
    2.)   _____

6. A written document that is signed by a person or a large
    number of people asking for something (See paragraph
    5.)   _____

7. Unwritten laws that have been developed through the
    years from old customs (See paragraph 6.)   _____

8. A person to whom one owes money (See paragraph 6.)   _____

9. The feeling of belonging by origin to one particular place
    OR parts of a plant that grows down in the soil in search
    of food and water (See paragraph 2.)   _____

10. A person who strongly believes in and fights for equality
    for women (See paragraph 7.)   _____

Match each word in Column A with the phrase in Column B that has a similar meaning. Write the number of the word next to the correct phrase.

A	**B**
1. encounter	_____ foreseeable
2. inane	_____ make fun of someone
3. predictable	_____ keep safe; guard
4. revise	_____ turn something around in the opposite direction
5. prosper	
6. protect	_____ meet
7. reverse	_____ senseless; silly
8. tease	_____ change
	_____ do well, especially in business

Choose four of the words from Column A above and write a sentence using each one.

1. _____

2. _____

3. _____

4. _____

Complete the following sentences about ideas in the reading, using your own words.

1. People who keep birth records are upset because _____

_____ .

2. Parents can name their new child _____

_____ .

3. Courts have pointed out that a person is free to choose _____

    _____ as long as _____

    _____ .

4. Although Mrs. Black _____ for several years, she

    still uses her _____ .

5. A woman named Cooperman went to court to have her named changed to

    Cooperperson because _____

    _____ .

Fill in the blanks in the following sentences with the appropriate words from this list:

adopt	registrar	dismay	automatically
grant	hyphenated	fraudulent	roots

1. In some cultures, a married woman is free to _____ her husband's name or to keep her own.

2. If a criminal changed his or her name for _____ purposes, it would not be legal.

3. Recordkeepers are reacting to name changes with _____ ; they are worried that people in the future will not be able to locate their _____ .

4. In many countries, the first-born son _____ takes the name of his father.

5. A university _____ keeps all school records, assigns class times and classrooms, and schedules examinations.

6. Words like *mother-in-law* and *self-starting* are _____ to show that these words function as one unit.

7. The judge refused to _____ Miss Cooperman's request to have her name changed.

Choose words from the list in the exercise above and use them or their related forms in sentences.

EXAMPLE: *The university registrar sent me an exam schedule.*

1. _____

2. _____

3. _____

Now change two of your sentences to express ideas opposite to those in the original sentences and write them below.

EXAMPLE: *The university registrar didn't send me an exam schedule.*

1. _____

2. _____

Follow-up Activities

1. Find the meaning of the following kinds of names. Give examples when you can.

a. Christian	**d.** given	**g.** middle	**j.** pen
b. family	**e.** maiden	**h.** nick-	**k.** pet
c. first	**f.** married	**i.** last	**l.** sur-

2. Identify some differences in names and naming customs between your country and another. Be prepared to report these differences to the class.

3. Many languages have words or word forms for the same job that differ depending on gender. English, for example, has actor and actress, waiter and waitress. List and compare gender words in your language with those in English. Compare your lists with those of other students.

4. Read this riddle and explain your answer to it.

   A father and son were in an auto accident. The father was killed and the son was taken to a hospital. In the operating room, the surgeon walked in and said, "I can't operate on this boy. He's my son." How is this possible?

   Read this riddle to some students or friends and find out who can guess the answer fastest.

The Right to Die

Before You Read

"The Right to Die" is a section of the book *Miller's Court*, a collection of discussions on legal issues by Arthur Miller, host of the TV program "Miller's Court."

This selection concerns a major contemporary legal problem. Since medical technology can keep sick people alive for a long time, is it legal for a doctor, a family, or a patient to stop treatment?

Think About It

Have you had any relatives or friends who have been terminally ill (whose illness is fatal) for a long time?

Who is responsible for deciding what should happen to very sick patients?

The Right to Die

Arthur Miller

1   Let's pose an unpleasant dilemma: Imagine that you're suffering from a terminal disease. You're in the hospital, where you're hooked up to a machine that keeps your vital organs functioning; without the machine you would quickly die of the illness's effects. You're also in constant pain, which is abated somewhat by injections of painkillers. The doctors tell you that the progress of the disease is irreversible and that you'll never recover — at most you have six months to live. They also inform you that the pain will get worse and worse, as your system becomes acclimated to the painkillers and as your condition degenerates.

2   Sound bad? Well, let's make it even worse. Let's say that the treatment you're receiving is extremely expensive. In addition to the usual high costs of hospitalization and medical care, there is the huge expense for using the machine that keeps you alive. Up to now your medical insurance has covered the costs, but soon they will exceed your coverage, and when that happens the expense is going to fall on your family. You have a wife and two children, and if you live for even another three or four months, you're going to leave them with staggering medical bills.

3   Under these circumstances, you might decide that you would prefer to have the machine that keeps you going disconnected so that you

can die naturally. But can you elect to do so? Is this a case in which you have a right to die? The answer is yes.

4   If you are terminally ill but mentally sound (in legal terms, you're "competent"), you can refuse a treatment that would prolong your life yet not offer any possibility of an actual cure. The distinction between "prolonging" and "curing" is significant. In our example, we've posited that you are connected to a machine that artificially keeps your body functioning but won't cure the disease. Thus you would have the legal right to ask that the machine be "unplugged," so that you could die naturally.

5   Note that to have the right to die, you must be "terminally ill." That means that the prognosis must be a matter of medical certitude — it clearly isn't enough that the doctors think that you *might* die, or even that you are *very likely* to die; rather, death must be inevitable. One might ask if this condition could ever be met, since there always seems to be a possibility, however remote, that a patient will recover, or that a cure for the disease will be developed before his time is up. Still, the possibility of either event occurring in certain cases is so unlikely that as a practical matter the situation is deemed hopeless, and the patient is allowed to refuse treatment.

6   Another requirement is that you not have long to live. In a sense, we are all terminal, since we will all die someday; what's unique about the terminal patient is that he is going to die of specified causes, and relatively soon. There's no exact time span that renders a disease terminal, but the six-month period in our example probably is short enough. Note that as the time period gets longer, we can't be sure that a cure won't be found, and so it's more difficult to conclude that recovery is impossible.

7   The right to die is based on two related legal doctrines. First, there is the centuries-old rule that everyone has a right of bodily self-determination. Simply stated, it's your body and as a general matter you can't be forced to accept medical treatment without your "informed consent." A doctor who violates this right (except in emergencies when there isn't time to get consent) commits a battery and can be sued by the patient. The second doctrine is the emerging constitutional right of bodily privacy. . . . Again, the idea is that you have a right to control what is done to your body and to be protected against unwanted physical intrusions upon it.

8   Now that you know some law, let's change the situation and test its limits. Suppose that you're terminally ill with cancer, and that at the most you have only two weeks to live. You're confined to a hospital bed, but you aren't being kept alive by any machines or treatment. You're in excruciating pain, which the doctors can do nothing about. Because you know there's no hope of recovery, because there's so little time anyway, and because you want to die a dignified death, you ask one of the doctors to give you a lethal injection that will end your life quickly and painlessly. Does your right to die entitle you to receive the shot?

9   The answer, as a legal matter, is a definite no. Moreover, anyone who gave you the injection could be put on trial for murder. This is mercy killing, and although juries often refuse to convict someone who does it, especially if the "killer" is a loved one of the patient, it continues to be viewed as criminal behavior.

10   Suppose that instead of giving you the injection, the doctor simply leaves a cup of poison on your nightstand with instructions for you to drink it "if you don't think you can hang on any longer." Again, this is illegal. Depending on the law of the state you're in, the doctor is subject to prosecution for abetting a suicide, or possibly for homicide; and you might be prosecuted for attempted suicide if you didn't die from the poison. Of course, it's extremely unlikely that any prosecutor would bring charges against you in this situation. . . . But regardless of whether you or your doctor would end up charged with a crime, the law's recognition of your right to die does not extend to getting the shot or being supplied with the poison.

11   Let's try one more variation. What if instead of being so open about helping you to die, the doctor was more subtle? Suppose he left a bottle of sleeping pills on the nightstand with instructions that you should be careful not to take more than two at a time, since if you took a lot you'd sleep permanently. Literally, all he's done is warn you against the dangers of overdose; arguably, however, he's instructed you on how to commit suicide — if you want to take the hint. Is this illegal? Presumably it is, if it can be shown that the doctor's intention was to help you to die. Realistically, however, it would be difficult to prove this to a jury, especially if they weren't anxious to convict the doctor in the first place.

12   The difference between the cases involving the injection, the poison, or the pills and our first example, in which you had the right to have treatment discontinued, is that there is an active intervention to bring about your death. The law distinguishes between these situations and one in which a treatment that is artificially *prolonging* a life simply is terminated. Stated another way, you have the right to be left alone to die a natural death, but you have no right to have the process speeded up.

Comprehension

1. What is mercy killing? Give an example to illustrate your answer.

2. Under what conditions does a person have the legal right to die?

3. What are the two legal doctrines on which the right to die is based?

4. In the reading, what are four ways to help a slowly dying patient end his life quickly?

5. In addition to suffering and pain, what other problems arise when a slowly dying patient is left to die naturally?

Discussion

1. Do you agree with the legal doctrines that are the basis for the right to die?

2. What is your opinion about the justification of mercy killing?

3. Would the situation be different if a patient refused a treatment that would cure him or her?

Language Practice

Substitute a word or phrase from the following list for an underlined word or phrase in the sentences below and rewrite the sentences.

disconnect	functioning	inevitable	lethal
excruciating	hooked up to	injection	mercy killing

1. You're in <u>very severe</u> pain, which the doctors can do nothing about.

   _____

2. Can you ask one of the doctors to give you a <u>deadly shot</u> that will end your life quickly and painlessly?

   _____

3. <u>Euthanasia</u>, ending a dying person's life quickly and painlessly, is viewed as criminal behavior by most courts of law.

   _____

4. You're <u>connected to</u> a machine that keeps your vital organs <u>working</u>.

   _____

5. If you were terminally ill, you would have the legal right to ask the doctor to <u>unplug</u> the machine that is keeping you alive.

   _____

6. To have the right to die, it isn't enough that the doctors think you might die; rather your death must be <u>sure to happen</u>.

   _____

When you are ill, often you have to ask the doctor or another person to do things for you. In other words, you can HAVE SOMEBODY DO SOMETHING for you. Complete the following sentences by writing an appropriate noun or verb from the list below in the blanks. You may use a word more than once.

Nouns		Verbs	
home	painkillers	disconnect	pay
company	sleeping pills	explain	prescribe
machine		give	send

1. If you are in pain, you can have the doctor _____ you

    _____ .

2. When you get a medical bill, you can have your insurance _____

    _____ the bill.

3. If you are terminally ill, you can have your lawyer _____ your

    rights to the doctor and you can have the doctor _____ the

    _____ which is prolonging your life.

4. If you find it difficult to sleep, you can have a doctor _____

    for you.

5. If you would rather die peacefully in your own bedroom, you can have the

    doctor _____ you _____ .

Complete the following sentences by using ideas from the reading. Include the words in brackets in your answers. Your choices should show that you understand the first part of each sentence.

1. In a sense, we are all terminal because someday we [die] _____ .

2. The doctors tell you that the progress of the disease is irreversible and that

    you [recover] _____ .

3.	If you are terminally ill but mentally "competent," you [refuse] _____

_____ .

4.	You have the right to be left alone to die a natural death, but you have

no [right, speed up] _____ .

5.	It's your body and [be forced] _____

_____ without your consent.

Read each sentence of the following paragraphs; then on the lines below them, write in your own words what the underlined words refer to or mean.

Up to now your medical insurance has covered the costs,[1] but soon they[2] will exceed your coverage, and when that[3] happens the expense is going to fall on your family.[4]

1.	the costs _____

2.	they _____

3.	that _____

4.	the expense is going to fall on your family _____

_____

Does your right to die entitle[1] you to receive a lethal[2] injection that will end your life quickly and painlessly? Definitely not. Moreover,[3] anyone who gave you the injection could be put on trial for murder. This[4] is mercy killing, and although juries often refuse to convict someone who does it,[5] especially if the "killer" is a loved one[6] of the patient, it[7] continues to be viewed as criminal behavior.

1.	entitle _____

2.	lethal _____

3.	Moreover _____

4.	This _____

5. it _____

6. a loved one _____

7. it _____

Using ideas from the reading, complete this paragraph.

There are several requirements you must meet to have the right to die.

_____

_____

_____

Follow-up Activities

1. Discover how death is defined: Look up the word in several dictionaries; ask a doctor; ask somebody who represents a religion; ask a lawyer. Then compare the definitions.

2. Conduct a poll by asking ten people this question: Should a doctor be allowed to end the life of a terminally ill patient if the patient and the family request it? Compare your results with those of other students.

3. Find out how medical insurance works in different countries, and compare the systems.

Chapter Review

1. This chapter concerns the rights of various people: passengers, children, the very ill. What other rights should people have? For example, consider these groups: customers; students; teachers.

2. Several readings in this chapter raise questions about individual rights as they conflict with the laws of a society. What do you think should be the basic rights of all people?

3. Consider some problems of law that have been created by modern technology. For example, as we build tall buildings, we prevent the sunlight from reaching nearby areas; do we all have a right to sunlight? We build machines that make a lot of noise (the Concorde airplane, for example); do we have a right to quiet?

Keeping Fit | **4**

One of the most popular topics in magazines and newspapers today is health. The readings in this chapter include reports on dangers to our health, the importance of diet, and even the role that pets may play in keeping people healthy.

New Findings on Longer Life

Before You Read

This selection, written by Karen Lehrman for *Consumers' Research* magazine, deals with recent medical findings about long life and personal health, cancer and work, geography and alcohol abuse. Lehrman supports her information with facts and statistics taken from medical journals, government and business studies, and university research.

Think About It

Can you think of reasons why some people always get sick or why some die at an early age?

Can sickness or an early death be avoided? How?

New Findings on Longer Life

Karen Lehrman

1 Within the last year medical breakthroughs have grabbed front-page headlines and incited nationwide debate at a seemingly unprecedented rate. Doctors implanted the second artificial heart, transferred the heart of a baboon into the chest of a premature infant, delivered the first frozen-embryo baby and identified the virus that is thought to cause the deadly AIDS. While these extraordinary developments absorb national attention, relatively minor studies and reports that more directly affect the average consumer sometimes go unnoticed.

2 The following items, culled from medical journals, government and business studies, and university research, will fill you in on some of the latest findings in the health field.

3 Once you're past a certain age, there's not much you can do to increase your lifespan. According to a new study in the *American Journal of Public Health,* starting a healthy diet and exercising regularly at age 65 or older will not necessarily affect your longevity.

4 Harvard University researchers found that of five personal-health practices — smoking, physical activity, alcohol consumption, hours of sleep and eating behavior — only one, smoking, is related to how long older people will live. Elderly women who have never smoked cigarettes will live longer than those who have, whereas among elderly men, there is no significant connection between health practices and mortality. The researchers do claim, however, that although they might not live longer, older people who switch over to healthy lifestyles will probably feel better and suffer fewer disabilities than those who continue with their unhealthy habits.

5 Among young and middle-aged adults, however, researchers are finding a relationship between personal health, disease and longevity. This new study emphasizes that you cannot generalize the findings on longevity to the elderly.

6 Men who spend a lot of time sitting down on the job are 60 percent more likely to get colon cancer than those whose jobs require a high level of activity, report researchers.

7 A new study out of the University of Southern California is the first to link the disease to lack of physical activity. Colon cancer, which kills 60,000 people annually, has already been linked to a low-fiber, high-fat diet.

8 The researchers analyzed 2,950 cases of colon cancer among men of different racial and economic groups and then divided the activity level of their occupations into three categories: sedentary jobs, including bookkeepers, bus drivers and computer programmers; moderate occupations, including salesmen, machinists and grade-school teachers; and high-activity jobs, including auto mechanics, plumbers and

longshoremen. Men in moderate-activity jobs had a 20 percent higher risk of getting colon cancer than men in high-activity occupations.

9   The researchers believe that physical activity stimulates the movement of wastes through the colon, thus reducing the time carcinogens are in contact with the colon lining.

10   Women were not included in the study because their occupations are less accurate measures of total activity.

11   The findings are consistent with the higher incidence of colon cancer in developed societies, says Dr. David Garabrant, the director of the study: "The transition from an agrarian, labor-intensive economy to an industrialized, capital-intensive economy is accompanied by broad shifts from physically active occupations to sedentary technical and managerial jobs."

12   People living in the Pacific states are twice as likely as people in other areas of the nation to die of cirrhosis of the liver as a result of heavy drinking, reports the Metropolitan Life Insurance Company. The national rate of death from the liver disease, however, has declined in the past decade.

13   Among those in the 35 to 74 age group, the death rates in 1980 were:

- Highest among men (53.3 per 100,000) and women (26.2 per 100,000) in the Pacific region — California, Washington, Oregon, Alaska and Hawaii. California had the highest rates of all among men (60 per 100,000), which was more than four times that of South Dakota (14.8 per 100,000). Among women, Nevada had the highest death rate (37.1 per 100,000) and Iowa, the lowest (7.4).
- Lowest among men (24.5 per 100,000) and women (10.6 per 100,000) in the West North Central part of the country — Minnesota, Iowa, Missouri, North Dakota, South Dakota, Nebraska and Kansas.
- Twenty-five percent greater than the national average in the District of Columbia, Nevada, New York and Rhode Island.
- Two-thirds or less than the national average in Idaho, Arkansas, Nebraska, Iowa, Kansas and Minnesota.

14   According to Dr. William Cunnick, medical director for Metropolitan Life, these state and regional differences can be explained by findings that indicate that the higher a state's socioeconomic status, the lower its death rates from cirrhosis, and the higher a state's unemployment rates, the higher its rate of alcohol abuse.

15   The overall rate of death from cirrhosis — including deaths under and over the 35 to 74 age group — declined from 15 per 100,000 in 1973 to 10.4 per 100,000 in 1982. About 28,000 people died from the liver disease in 1983.

Comprehension

Expand your understanding of the article's main ideas.

1. According to a new study in *The American Journal of Public Health,* what have researchers found out about the life spans of young adults, middle-aged adults, and elderly people? What may prolong the life of an elderly person?

2. What major factor has been linked to colon cancer? Who is more likely to get this type of cancer?

3. Would colon cancer be more prevalent in a developed or a developing country? Explain your answer.

4. What seems to be the relationship between cirrhosis of the liver and certain regions of the United States?

5. This article appeared in a magazine for "consumers." Articles on health fill newspapers and magazines in the United States. How do people usually get information on recent advances in health in your country?

Applications

Relate the article to events in your own life.

1. Describe the most recent medical breakthrough or research with which you are familiar.

2. How much is health related to factors such as social status, education, employment, activity, diet, and so on? Choose a factor with which you are familiar and describe it.

3. Are the social problems that affect health (such as drinking and smoking) common in your country? Are they considered health problems? Why or why not?

4. "An ounce of prevention is worth a pound of cure." What can governments do to help prevent health problems? What can you do to prevent illness and prolong life?

Pets

Before You Read

Tom Ferguson, a doctor, wrote this article for a health magazine. He believes the day is coming when doctors may be able to prescribe pets instead of pills for their patients.

Think About It

Do you think a pet could help you stay healthy or feel better?

Do any of your friends have pets? What kinds?

Pets

Tom Ferguson, M.D.

1 Is it possible that a dog leaping and barking with joy when you return home, a cat curled and purring in your lap, or a fish swimming peacefully in a tank can reduce your blood pressure, alter the course of heart disease, and decrease your stress level? Recent studies suggest they can do this and more. "I believe the day is coming when doctors will sometimes 'prescribe' pets instead of pills," says Dr. Leo Bustad, dean of the College of Veterinary Medicine at Washington State University. "What pill gives so much love, makes its owner feel safe, stimulates laughter, encourages regular exercise, and makes a person feel needed?"

PETS AND HEART DISEASE

2   When University of Pennsylvania researchers studied a group of seriously ill heart patients, they found that pet owners had much better survival records. In the year the study lasted, the death rate for patients who did not own pets was 28 percent. Pet owners had a death rate of less than six percent.

3   Another study looked at the effects of pets on older people. A British psychologist gave a parakeet to each of a group of elders. Members of the control group got a begonia. After five months there was a noticeable increase in health and morale among the pet owners. Swedish researchers found that 15 percent of the elderly persons studied considered their pet to be their most significant social contact.

4   Other health effects have also been documented: Petting the soft fur of a dog or cat can profoundly lower blood pressure. Watching fish

in a tank is for many people as effective a way of relaxing minds and bodies as any tranquilizer or meditative technique.

5   A number of studies suggest that people who own pets are generally in better health than those who do not. These positive effects seem to hold for every kind of pet studied so far, including — but not limited to — dogs, cats, gerbils, parakeets, chickens, iguanas, fish, mice, and rabbits.

6   The researchers who performed the study of heart disease patients mentioned above, concluded that having a pet decreased risk of dying by about 3 percent per year. This would put pet-owning in roughly the same category as such other health-promoting behaviors as eating a healthy diet, exercising regularly, managing stress, not smoking, being in a committed couple relationship, and having close ties with family and friends.

7   Among other benefits, our pets provide us with an intimate bond with another living being. Such bonds — like the intimacy of close human relationships — seem to produce a kind of anti-stress armor which protects us from the effects of a variety of life stresses that might otherwise predispose us to illness.

URBAN RESIDENTS, MEN BENEFIT MOST

8   Studies show that city dwellers benefit most from being pet owners, probably because urbanites usually have more personalized connection to their animals. It's not just the presence of a pet that enhances our health, it's the quality of the relationship.

9   Men benefit more from owning pets than women. This is probably because men have fewer outlets for intimacy and touch, and thus have more need of an animal to help them express and receive affection. Men touch other people far less frequently than women do, but they touch pets as much or more.

PETS AS FAMILY

10   University of Maryland researcher Dr. Ann Cain found that 87 percent of pet owners thought of their pets as members of the family. Eighty-one percent felt that pets tuned into their feelings, and 38 percent celebrated their pet's birthday.

11   Pets can help bring families together by promoting interaction among family members, by relieving stress of busy parents and growing children, by helping children learn the importance of responsibility and discipline. Even a pet's death can serve to bring family members closer together. "Shared feelings of grief can form a strong family bond," says Dr. Michael Fox, scientific director of the Humane Society of the United States, "uniting children and parents in love and respect."

12   Many older people feel a need for more love and affection than they receive. "Companion animals may be a significant source of warmth, affection, love and devotion," Dr. Bustad writes. "In some

cases animals are the *only* source. In many cases a pet becomes a person's reason for living."

UNCONDITIONAL LOVE

13   Animals make few emotional demands. Their affection does not depend on our reaching a sales quota, meeting a deadline, or keeping the house spotless. They do not worship youth or beauty, and they care nothing for financial or social success. Where a human confidant might analyze our problems, offer advice, or volunteer opinions, our dog will climb into our lap and lick our face.

14   Pets help us relax because they love us for who we are. Just our presence is enough. Pet owners say they like their pets best when they return home and receive an enthusiastic greeting.

HELPING US THROUGH HARD TIMES

15   Because of the intimacy and involvement they provide, pets can be especially valuable when we are experiencing major life transitions — a move to a new home, unemployment, illness, severe depression, the breakup of a relationship, the death of a loved one, or other serious losses or disruptions. Veterinarian Bruce Fogle writes of a young man living alone for the first time who named his cat "Mom."

16   Our pets' continuing affection assures us that we are still lovable, that our essence has not changed. This makes pets especially useful in the treatment of the chronically ill.

PETS AS THERAPISTS

17   Animals can often help those who can no longer be helped by other people; in particular, pets can help people who feel withdrawn, depressed, or hopeless. Emotionally disturbed children who refuse to interact with human therapists will frequently become very involved with a dog and may even confide in it. Once the child and the dog have begun to play, the therapist may be able to join in. Child and therapist may later go on to form a direct relationship.

PETS AND STRESS

18   The dog who greets us at homecoming or a cat who chases a bit of string or hides in an empty paper bag provides us with an invitation to laugh, relax, and enjoy ourselves. The blood pressures of hypertensive patients dropped considerably while watching tropical fish. Looking at fish tanks has also helped anxious patients relax before oral surgery.

19   Nursing homes have discovered the therapeutic value of bringing pets to residents. Pet adoption and pet visitation programs are now under way in cities across the country. Call your local Humane Society or Society for the Prevention of Cruelty to Animals (SPCA) for information on local programs.

SOMEONE TO CARE FOR

20   The task of caring for a pet is often a child's first serious responsibility. Throughout our lives our pets pull us back into the daily rounds of the natural world with their needs for continuing care.

21   Feeding the cat, bathing the dog, tending the fish tank, taking the parakeet on your finger — these little acts of caring assure the caregiver that he or she is truly needed. Such feelings can at times serve as a literal lifeline.

22   The child who once fed the dog may many years later have little strength or opportunity to help another human being. But he or she can still continue the life-giving rituals of caring by tending a single goldfish in a bowl, providing a saucer of milk for a stray cat, or putting out crumbs for the winter birds.

Comprehension

1.   What evidence is there that pets affect their owners' health?

2.   What aspects of human health seem to be affected by pet ownership?

3.   How do different groups benefit to different degrees by having pets?

4.   In what different ways do people benefit from pets?

Discussion

1.   How do you feel about pets?

2.   Do you think that people ever treat animals better than they treat other people? Give examples to support your answer.

3.   Do you feel that baby animals are good gifts for children? Explain your answer.

4.   How has this article changed your opinion about pets?

Language Practice

If you think a statement below is true, put a T in the blank next to it. If you think a statement is false, put an F.

According to this article, a pet . . .

1. _____ makes many demands on its owner.

2. _____ is just as important as a good diet, not smoking, and exercise.

3. _____ benefits women more than men.

4. _____ can allow a man to be more intimate.

5. _____ is sometimes the only source of companionship for the elderly.

6. _____ can reduce one's blood pressure but not decrease one's stress level.

7. _____ can be a nuisance in a nursing home.

8. _____ is often considered to be a member of the family.

9. _____ is less popular among people who live in cities.

10. _____ might receive a present from its owner on its birthday.

After you correct the true or false exercise above, reread the false statements. Correct the false statements by writing the correct information on the lines below.

_____

_____

_____

_____

Rewrite each sentence below, substituting words or phrases with a similar meaning for the underlined words. Do not use a dictionary.

1. Researchers studied the <u>effects</u> of pets on older people. (See paragraph 3.)

_____

2. The researchers who studied heart disease patients with pets found that having a pet <u>decreased</u> the <u>risk</u> of dying. (See paragraph 6.)

_____

3. Our pets provide us with an <u>intimate bond</u> with another living being. (See paragraph 7.)

_____

4. A pet's <u>affection</u> does not depend on our doing a good job at the office or keeping the house <u>spotless</u>. (See paragraph 13.)

_____

5. Pets <u>provide</u> us with an invitation to laugh, relax, and enjoy ourselves. (See paragraph 18.)

_____

For each of the following verbs, first write its definition, and then write sentences using it that answer the questions on the left, as in the example below.

protect   worship   refuse   interact   confide

EXAMPLE: flee

Definition: *to run away*
               to escape

Who? What?   *People who are in trouble flee.*
              Animals flee from danger.

Where?   *Refugees flee from one country to*
          another. Criminals flee from
          prison

When?   *Children flee when they're afraid.*
         Some criminals flee at night.

Why?   *Some people flee because they're not*
        happy. In the 1920s, immigrants fled
        Europe to find a better place to live.

WORD: protect

Definition: _____

Who? What?   _____

               _____

Where?   _____

                          _____

When?   _____

                          _____

Why?   _____

                          _____

Do the other words on another piece of paper.

Find the meaning of the underlined words in the following sentences. Then rewrite each sentence, substituting words or phrases that express the same idea as the underlined ones.

EXAMPLE: Researchers found that <u>pet owners had much better survival records.</u>

Researchers found that *people who had pets lived longer.*

1. Researchers concluded that having a pet <u>benefitted</u> more men than women. (See paragraph 9.)

    _____

    _____

2. <u>Urbanites</u> usually <u>have more personalized connection to</u> their animals. (See paragraph 8.)

    _____

    _____

3. Eighty-one percent of pet owners felt that pets <u>tuned into their feelings.</u> (See paragraph 10.)

    _____

    _____

4. Pets do not <u>worship youth or beauty</u>, and they <u>care nothing for financial or social success</u>. (See paragraph 13.)

_____

_____

5. A dog who <u>greets us at homecoming</u> loves us for what we are. (See paragraph 18.)

_____

_____

6. Nursing homes have <u>discovered the therapeutic value of bringing pets to residents</u>. (See paragraph 19.)

_____

_____

Fill in the blanks below with appropriate words from this list:

    alter   benefit   document   lower   promote   protect

1. Petting the soft fur of a dog or cat can profoundly _____ blood pressure.

2. Studies show that city dwellers _____ most from being pet owners.

3. Researchers can _____ the many positive health effects of owning a pet.

4. Taking care of a dog could _____ the course of a patient's heart disease, from very serious to remarkably improved.

5. Researchers have shown that pets can _____ us from the effects of a variety of stresses.

6. A healthy diet and regular exercise as well as pet ownership all _____ good health behavior(s).

In the article we find this sentence: "It's not just the presence of a pet that enhances our health, it's [also] the quality of the relationship." Use this sentence pattern to comment on other kinds of experiences.

EXAMPLE: *It's not just studying grammar that improves your English, it's also practicing it as often as possible.*

1. _____

2. _____

3. _____

4. _____

Write five sentences, using a verb and a noun from the following lists in each sentence.

Verb	Noun
confide	individual
enhance	health
leap	lap
reduce	risk
relieve	stress

1. _____

2. _____

3. _____

4. _____

5. _____

Choose a noun and verb according to the directions in the brackets in the sentence below. Then write four or five sentences to complete the paragraph.

[Supply any individual] benefit(s) more from [verb + ing] than . . .

_____

_____

_____

_____

_____

Supply a noun for the sentence below. Then write four or five sentences to complete the paragraph.

People who [supply any activity] are generally in better health than those

who do not. _____

_____

_____

_____

_____

Follow-up Activities

1. Look up these words in a dictionary if you do not know their meaning. Be ready to explain how they are related to pets.

   breed   neutered   train
   groom   pedigree   vaccination
   kennel   puppy   veterinarian
   kitten   stray

2. Consult your classmates about people and pets in their countries. Ask these questions:
   a. Are pets popular in your country? If the answer is no, why not?
   b. What are the most popular pets?
   c. How do people treat their pets?
   d. What kind of names do people give their pets?

3. Dogs can respond to commands. To what commands would you want your dog to respond? Make a list and compare it with those of other students. (Remember that dogs respond only to short commands.)

4. There are special breeds of dogs for special purposes. Find out (by consulting classmates, teachers, friends, or reference materials) which ones are used for: (a) the blind, (b) skiers, (c) hunters, (d) police/army, (e) protection.

5. The Humane Society and the Society for the Prevention of Cruelty to Animals (SPCA) are mentioned in the article. Find out what these societies do.

6. Pretend that you work in a pet store and you have to write two advertisements (for a newspaper, radio, or TV), one selling pets to children, the other to the elderly. Include information about the pets and about how they can benefit people. You might get some ideas and language from the ads below.

PETS

BICHON FRISE, neutered male, 2 years old. Free to good home. Friendly, affectionate, good with pets/children. Needs attention.

CHARMING, NEUTERED, FULLY-VACCINATED 6-mo. male kitten. Loves outdoor freedom. Sleeps all night. Playful, mild, affectionate disposition. No trouble. Tiger with white lower face, chest and paws. FREE.

NOVA: Handsome, sweet-natured, well-behaved small "shepherd." Neutered male. Owned by ill priest, needs new home.

ALL BLACK adult female cat needs good home. (Has had all necessary veterinary care.)

LHASA APSO PUPPIES. Champion sired, home raised, loveable, friendly temperment, health guaranteed. 2 free groomings given $325–$350.

FREE — 3 adorable kittens looking for kind homes. (2 calico, 1 grey stripes).

DOG ORPHANS INC. Offers Dogs and Puppies that make friendly healthy family pets. Choose pure and mixed breeds from a non-profit Humane Society. Donations from $25 up, including inoculation.

TROPICLAND PET SHOP - Largest and most complete Pet Shop in this area. Tropical fish, aquariums, parakeets, and small animals.

Topics for Further Discussion or Writing

1. How does a pet bring us into closer touch with the natural world?

2. As the world population increases, there is less room for wild animals. Do you know of any attempts to preserve the world's wild animals?

3. This article stresses the benefits of pets. What are some disadvantages of having pets?

4. Animals communicate in different ways. What are some of these ways? What words do you have in your language to describe some animal sounds?

5. We frequently use references to animals to express ideas in interesting ways. For example, we may say, "He eats like a bird" or "like a pig." What are some similar expressions in your language? Compare them with expressions in English.

A Guide to Better Health

Before You Read

This article on diets and health was written for *Bostonia* magazine by Dr. Joseph Vitale and science writer Robert Ross.

Think About It

What kinds of foods do you like to eat? Are there any foods you avoid for health or diet reasons?

Do you do any physical activity every day?

A Guide to Better Health

Joseph Vitale, M.D., and Robert Ross

1   Whatever you eat, you are on a diet. The trick of eating well is to find the right diet. That diet is a simple one: eat appropriate amounts of foods taken from the four basic food groups.

2   Nutrition, health and lifestyle are related by a simple equation: weight gained or lost equals the difference between energy taken in and energy spent. When more energy is taken into the body than it can burn, some of that energy is stored through the body in the form of fat. When the body needs more energy than the diet is supplying, the body converts some of that stored fat to energy.

3   For some reason, this equation is too simple to suit the tastes of most Americans. We want something to make it more complicated. But that is all there is to it. To lose weight, exercise more or eat less.

CHOOSING THE PROPER DIET

4   Picking a proper diet is the first and most important step toward losing weight. Naturally the diet must supply fewer calories than you normally need so that your body can get the rest of the fuel it needs from the fat you have stored. But this does not mean that your diet must be so Spartan that you fail to get the essential nutrients you need. A weight-loss diet should limit the number of calories but not at the expense of nutrients you need.

5   An adequate diet for losing weight must take off no more than one or two pounds a week. It must also
   • allow some foods you like to eat;
   • maintain normal health;
   • remain satisfying for several months;

- not require special foods or gadgets;
- draw upon the four food groups;
- suit your personal budget.

In addition, while on this diet, you should try to learn new ways of preparing food so that the old fattening habits are replaced by new, lower-caloric ways of preparing food.

The Basic Four Food Groups

Food	Amount per Serving	Servings per Day
Meat Group		
Meat, lean	2 to 3 ounces cooked	2 (can be eaten as mixtures of
Poultry	2 to 3 ounces	animal and vegetable foods;
Fish	2 to 3 ounces	if only vegetable protein is
Hard cheese	2 to 3 ounces	consumed, it must be
Eggs	2 to 3	balanced protein)
Cottage cheese	½ cup	
Dry beans and peas	1 to 1½ cups cooked	
Nuts and seeds	½ to ¾ cup	
Peanut butter	4 tablespoons	
Milk Group		
Milk	8 ounces (1 cup)	2, children, teenagers,
Yogurt, plain	1 cup	pregnant women and nursing
Hard cheese	1¼ ounces	mothers require additional
Cheese spread	2 ounces	servings
Ice cream	1½ cups	
Cottage cheese	2 cups	
Bread and Cereal Group		
Bread	1 slice	4, whole grain or enriched
Cooked cereal	½ to ¾ cup	only, including at least one
Pasta	½ to ¾ cup	serving of whole grain
Rice	½ to ¾ cup	
Dry cereal	1 ounce	
Vegetable and Fruit Group		
Vegetables, cut up	½ cup	4, including one good
Fruits, cut up	½ cup	vitamin C source
Grapefruit	½ medium	
Melon	½ medium	
Orange	1	
Potato	1 medium	
Salad	1 bowl	
Lettuce	1 wedge	

These amounts were established by the U.S. Department of Agriculture to meet specific nutritional requirements.

Recommended Daily Dietary Allowances for Energy*

	Age Years	Weight kg	Weight lb	Energy kcal
Infants	0.0–0.5	6	14	kg × 117
	0.5–1.0	9	20	kg × 108
Children	1–3	13	28	1300
	4–6	20	44	1800
	7–10	30	66	2400
Males	11–14	44	97	2800
	15–18	61	134	3000
	19–22	67	147	3000
	23–50	70	154	2700
	51 +	70	154	2400
Females	11–14	44	97	2400
	15–18	54	119	2100
	19–22	58	128	2100
	23–50	58	128	2000
	51 +	58	128	1800
Pregnancy				+ 300
Lactation				+ 500

*Food and Nutrition Board: *Recommended Dietary Allowances,* National Academy of Sciences–National Research Council, Washington, D.C., 1974.

6   As important as the food you take in is the energy you burn. Building new activities into your life to increase your activity levels is an important part of losing weight, for once the new activities and the new ways of eating become firmly rooted habits, you will take off the weight and keep it off.

TO INCREASE ACTIVITY LEVEL

7   Too often people embark on an exercise program, lose weight, but make no changes in their old habits. As a matter of fact, this is why most of the commercial quick-loss diet programs fail. They manage to motivate people to change their habits for a short time, but not for the long haul.

8   Activity all adds up so anything you can do to add steps or increase the work load, even in simple ways, eventually makes a difference:

- walking to work instead of driving;
- parking the car at the far end of the parking lot;
- walking up stairs rather than taking the elevator;
- doing errands yourself rather than sending others;
- keeping all sports and recreational equipment working and available.

Every activity takes energy. The more energy you spend on these activities, the less goes into storage as fat. Every 3500 calories burned and not replenished by eating is a pound of fat lost.

9   It takes quite a bit of activity to add up to 3500 calories. The following table shows the number of calories burned per minute of doing various activities.

Calories Used per Minute During Activity

Activity	Weight in Pounds						
	100	120	150	170	200	220	250
Badminton	4.3	5.2	6.5	7.4	8.7	9.6	10.9
Bicycling, 5.5 mph	3.1	3.8	4.7	5.3	6.3	6.9	7.9
Bicycling, 10 mph	5.4	6.5	8.1	9.2	10.8	11.9	13.6
Calisthenics	3.3	3.9	4.9	5.6	6.6	7.2	8.2
Canoeing, 4 mph	4.6	5.6	7.0	7.9	9.3	10.2	11.6
Golf	3.6	4.3	5.4	6.1	7.2	7.9	9.0
Handball	6.3	7.6	9.5	10.7	12.7	13.9	15.8
Mountain climbing	6.6	8.0	10.0	11.3	13.3	14.6	16.6
Jogging, 11-min. mile	6.1	7.3	9.1	10.4	12.2	13.4	15.3
Running, 8-min. mile	9.4	11.3	14.1	16.0	18.8	20.7	23.5
Running, 5-min. mile	13.1	15.7	19.7	22.3	26.3	28.9	32.8
Racquetball	6.3	7.6	9.5	10.7	12.7	13.9	15.8
Skating, moderate	3.6	4.3	5.4	6.1	7.2	7.9	9.0
Skiing, downhill	6.3	7.6	9.5	10.7	12.7	13.9	15.8
Skiing, cross-country	7.2	8.7	10.8	12.3	14.5	15.9	18.0
Squash	6.8	8.1	10.2	11.5	13.6	14.9	17.0
Swimming, breaststroke	4.8	5.7	7.2	8.1	9.6	10.5	12.0
Swimming, crawl	5.8	6.9	8.7	9.8	11.6	12.7	14.5
Table tennis	2.7	3.2	4.0	4.6	5.4	5.9	6.8
Tennis	4.5	5.4	6.8	7.7	9.1	10.0	11.4
Volleyball, moderate	2.3	2.7	3.4	3.9	4.6	5.0	5.7
Walking, 3 mph	2.7	3.2	4.0	4.6	5.4	5.9	6.8
Walking, 4 mph	3.9	4.6	5.8	6.6	7.8	8.5	9.7

Developed under standardized conditions at the Human Performance Research Center at Brigham Young University in Provo, Utah.

WHAT DOES YOUR BODY DO WITH THE ENERGY?

10   The calories of energy liberated from food are used for three important functions of the body.

11   First, calories provide the energy to keep the body working. Even when you are resting, your body needs energy for breathing, circulation of the blood, digestion and the many chemical reactions going on in the body all the time. This basic level of energy needed to keep the body at the resting state is known as the basal metabolic rate.

12   Second, calories provide energy needed for activity. People who are physically active need more calories of fuel than people who are

relatively sedentary. *Sedentary* lifestyles are those that keep a person chained to a desk eight hours a day with no other physical activity. Also, people who are confined because of illness or disability lead sedentary lives. *Moderate* activity levels are those in which a person works at a sedentary job but makes the time for regular moderate exercise. Jogging a few miles a day three or four times a week, doing housework or playing a friendly game of squash are all examples of moderate activity levels. *Active* lifestyles involve daily hard work or physical training.

13   Third, calories provide the energy needed for growth. Infants, children and adolescents need far more energy for their size than do adults because their bodies are still growing rapidly. This growth requires considerable energy. Adults are not growing as rapidly. Some cells are being continuously replaced and other routine maintenance functions are going on, but adults do not need the great amounts of energy for growth and maintenance that children require. As a result, adults who eat as they did when they were younger, find themselves growing fatter.

How Many Calories Do You Burn?

To compute the number of calories you burn during the course of a day, use the following form.

Age: _____ years   Height: _____ inches

Present body weight: _____ pounds or _____ kilograms
(Divide your body weight in pounds by 2.2)

Desirable weight range: _____ pounds or _____ kilograms
Before filling out the form, calculate the number of minutes per day you spend sleeping; lying awake; sitting; doing light activity; and doing light, moderate, heavy, severe, and very severe exercise. This should total 1440 minutes.

Energy Level	Energy Spent (cal/kg/minute)	Number of Minutes Spent at That Level	Energy Spent (per 1 kg body weight)
Sleeping	0 000	×	=
Lying awake	0 002	×	=
Sitting	0 005	×	=
Light activity	0 015	×	=
Light exercise	0 025	×	=

Energy Level	Energy Spent (cal/kg/minute)	Number of Minutes Spent at That Level	Energy Spent (per 1 kg body weight)
Moderate exercise	0 040	×	=
Heavy exercise	0 065	×	=
Severe exercise	0 105	×	=
Very severe exercise	0 140	×	=
Stairs (down)	0 012	× _____ (number of flights)	=
Stairs (up)	0 036	× _____ (number of flights)	=

Total minutes _____ (should be 1440)   Total energy in 24 hours

Total energy spent on muscular activities for the day equals the figure per kilogram you just derived, times the total kilograms of your body weight. (To get your body weight in kilograms, divide your weight in pounds by 2.2.)

Energy spent on muscular activities in 24 hours = _____ cal/kg

× _____ kg

= _____ cal

LIFESTYLE

14   How people eat is often determined by their lifestyle. The person who rushes from the office to pick up a three-piece fried chicken dinner at Colonel Sanders picks up 1070 calories. Add a large chocolate Dairy Queen malt to that and there is another 830 calories. If breakfast that morning was a couple of filled Danish with coffee and cream, that was another 500 or 600 calories.

15   There are many problems with eating this way. Leaving aside the fact that eating on the run is no fun and that it does not allow the time to relax and enjoy the food and companionship of a quiet meal, this kind of eating is bad nutrition. These meals buy their necessary nutrients at the cost of a great number of calories.

16   Nutritionists have developed the concept of *nutrient density* to compare the nutritional quality of different meals. Nutrient density is the amount of nutrients per number of calories. With respect to vitamin C, for instance, tomato juice has a higher nutrient density than orange juice. That is, a glass of tomato juice gives more vitamin C at fewer calories than does a glass of orange juice.

17   The problem with living a lifestyle that relies heavily on fast foods chosen indiscriminately is that it is a diet style heavy on empty calories.

18   Fancier restaurants pose other problems. The goal of a good restaurant, after all, is to delight you with beautifully prepared, appetizing foods. The table setting, the service, the way food is arranged on the plate, the selection of foods and wines and, of course, the fabulous desserts, are all designed to make people break their firmest resolves to eat sensibly. The whole presentation of the food is calculated to say, "Eat. Eat."

19   Then, too, if the dinner is going to cost $30 a person, we feel that we must eat all of it, from the cream soup, rich buttery sauce and pommes Anna, to the ginger cheesecake for dessert.

20   The point of knowing something about nutrition is to be able to choose wisely. Rich desserts taste good and there is no need to give them up entirely. But with some attention to weight and the rest of nutrition-related health, you can put together a prudent diet that has enough foods drawn from the basic four food groups and has fun foods in moderation.

You will know that you are eating wisely if:
- you are healthy;
- your weight remains fairly constant;
- you have enough energy to get you through the day;
- you are physically active;
- you enjoy eating and have a good appetite.

Comprehension

1. What are the basic food groups?

2. What is the equation that relates nutrition and weight?

3. What characterizes an adequate diet for losing weight?

4. What is the recommended number of energy calories for a twenty-year-old male?

5. Why should people who want to diet increase their activity?

6. If you weigh 150 pounds, what activities could you do to lose one pound? For how long would you have to do these activities?

7. What are the three functions of calories?

8. Why is eating fast foods a nutritional problem?

Discussion

1. Do you eat foods from all the basic four food groups every day?

2. Which of the life styles described in the reading do you have now? If you have changed your life style recently, have you also changed your diet?

3. To what extent are nutrition and diets discussed in newspapers and magazines in your country?

4. If you don't live at home, compare the way you eat now with the way you ate when you lived at home.

5. How important is eating for you? Do you plan meals carefully?

6. Is it possible for most people in your country to get foods from the four groups? What kinds of foods are most available at a low cost?

Language Practice

Find out the meaning of the underlined words below. Then rewrite each sentence substituting appropriate words or phrases for the underlined ones.

1. The trick of eating well is to find the right diet. (See paragraph 1.)

   _____

2. Nutrition, health, and life style are related by a simple equation: weight gained or lost equals the difference between energy taken in and energy spent. (See paragraph 2.)

   _____

   _____

   _____

3. When the body needs more energy than the diet is supplying, the body converts some of that stored fat to energy. (See paragraph 2.)

   _____

   _____

4. Picking a proper diet is an important step toward losing weight. (See paragraph 4.)

   _____

5. An adequate diet must <u>maintain</u> normal health and <u>suit</u> your personal budget. (See paragraph 5.)

_____

_____

6. Too often people <u>embark</u> on an exercise program but make no changes in their old habits. (See paragraph 7.)

_____

_____

7. The <u>goal</u> of a good restaurant is to <u>delight</u> you with appetizing foods. (See paragraph 18.)

_____

8. With some attention to weight and nutrition, you can <u>put together</u> a <u>prudent</u> diet. (See paragraph 20.)

_____

_____

With which of the situations described in the right-hand column can you associate the sentences below? Circle the correct answer in the right-hand column.

1. A weight-loss diet should limit the number of calories but not at the expense of nutrients you need.

    a. Tomato juice has a higher nutrient density than orange juice so it gives more vitamin C at fewer calories.

    b. He knew that eating ice cream every night would be bad for his weight, but he did it anyway.

    c. The computer cost $2500 in the store, but she bought one from a friend for $1500.

2. Eating on the run is no fun.

    a. A medical student often gets up at 5:00 A.M., goes to the hospital at 6:00, visits patients till 7:30, attends a lecture till 8:30, works in the operating room from 8:30 to 12:00, and so on.

    b. John decided to enter the bicycle race from Paris to Monaco.

    c. It was a long baseball game, but the Yankees won 8–7.

Think of someone with different tastes in food from yours. Make a comparison by choosing a meal (breakfast, lunch, or dinner) and listing the foods below. Is one diet better than the other? Why?

You   **Someone else**

_____ _____   _____ _____

_____ _____   _____ _____

Think of someone who wears a style of clothing different from yours. Compare what you might wear with what that person might wear. Show your list to others to see which they prefer.

You   **Someone else**

_____ _____   _____ _____

_____ _____   _____ _____

Find out what *gadgets* means. Then list three gadgets below; compare your list with those of other students.

_____   _____   _____

Almost every country has fast foods (inexpensive foods that can be bought easily, often on the street, and consumed quickly). What are some common fast foods available in your country? List them below.

_____   _____   _____

Choose foods from the basic four food groups. On the lines below, write
three or four sentences describing what you would like to eat during a typical
day. Begin with "For breakfast, I would like . . ."

_____

_____

_____

Describe the activities you do every day that burn energy. Begin the paragraph with "In the morning, I . . ."

_____

_____

_____

_____

Write two or three sentences that describe a process in which something is
changed into something else. See the equation in paragraph 2 for an example.
Another example might be what happens when we boil water.

_____

_____

_____

Write a paragraph that describes the three functions of calories of energy.
Use your own words as much as possible.

_____

_____

_____

_____

Study the chart on calories used per minute in the reading. On the lines below, describe the activities you would choose and the amount of time necessary for you to lose one pound.

_____

_____

_____

_____

_____

_____

Follow-up Activities

1. Use the "How Many Calories Do You Burn" chart to compute the number of calories you burn during the course of a day. Compare your results with those of other students.

2. Ask three people what they ate yesterday. Be prepared to describe their diets in terms of the basic four food groups.

3. Find an article on food or diet in a current magazine or newspaper and be prepared to report on it.

4. Some people eat just to get energy; they eat to live. Others like food very much; they live to eat. For others, eating is a social event. Describe the attitudes of members of your family (or of a group of friends) toward eating.

_____

Update on Successes of Biofeedback

Before You Read

This article describes current research in biofeedback, which can help a person detect very small changes in body physiology. Recognizing these changes, a person can learn to control certain body functions to eliminate or reduce pains such as migraine headaches.

Think About It

Do you sometimes experience a bad headache, backache, or other physical discomfort?

What do you usually do for yourself when you are in pain?

Do you know when you are going to feel bad? How do you know?

Update on Successes of Biofeedback

Anne C. Highland, Ph.D.

1   When biofeedback first made headlines, it generated high hopes. It seemed as if technology had at last come to rescue us from pain and suffering. When these hopes crashed, as all unrealistic hopes must, then biofeedback was dismissed as just another expensive toy.

2   Meanwhile, serious research was going on, with unglamorous data analysis and follow-up studies. Now we can evaluate what biofeedback is and what it is not. Contrary to popular belief, biofeedback instruments do not change the body's functioning; instead, they monitor it. Biofeedback is a form of teaching. Using biofeedback, we can become sensitive to subtle body signals arising from very slight changes in our own physiology. Once we are aware of these signals, we can learn to control certain body functions so as to lose a painful symptom or to regain a lost ability.

3   Although biofeedback has proven effective in helping people gain control over a variety of physiological functions formerly thought to be purely involuntary, its greatest use at present seems to be in treating stress-related ailments. Research suggests that people who have headaches, high blood pressure, jaw clenching (bruxism), or muscle spasms as a result of prolonged stress are likely to be helped by biofeedback therapy if they are willing to take an active role in regaining and maintaining good health. Biofeedback alone teaches the person how to gain voluntary control over the symptom, and the therapeutic procedures that often accompany biofeedback help the person become aware of why the problem occurred and how such problems might be prevented in the future.

4   There are several types of biofeedback equipment, all of which monitor body signals and feed information about extremely small changes in body functioning back to the patient either by an auditory signal, consisting of a variable tone or set of beeps, or by a visual display, which is often a light bar that fluctuates with the body signal being measured.

5   The most common biofeedback instrument is the electromyograph, or EMG, which measures muscle tension. Three electrodes,

two active electrodes and one ground, are placed on the surface of the skin, held in place by adhesive tape or an adjustable band. For headache control, electrodes are usually placed either on the forehead or near the back of the neck. For other problems, such as spasms in the lower back, electrodes may either be placed on the particular muscle or be attached to both wrists, where they monitor the tension in a large group of muscles of the torso.

6   EMG biofeedback is usually used to teach a person how to relax a muscle or muscle group when excessive tension causes unpleasant symptoms. However, it also is being used in some rehabilitation centers for the opposite problem: in cases of paralysis, when there is some residual function in the muscle, biofeedback can help the patient learn how to increase the tension of the muscle and sometimes even regain use of the muscle.

7   Another common biofeedback instrument is the temperature trainer. A small sensor is fastened by adhesive to the body, usually to a fingertip. The temperature trainer is sensitive to temperature changes of hundredths of a degree, so the patient can become aware of extremely slight changes in finger temperature. This sensitivity makes it easier to learn to warm the hands.

8   Changing the temperature in parts of our bodies may sound impossible until we consider that our blood vessels are surrounded by tiny muscles. If they are contracted, the blood flow to that organ or part of the body is reduced; if they are relaxed, the blood flow increases. The tension in these tiny muscles is not usually under voluntary control, although there are scientifically documented reports of the ability of certain Indian yogis who have gained this kind of control over parts of their circulatory systems. Temperature training with biofeedback can give a person voluntary control of this normally involuntary function.

9   People under chronic stress may find that their hands are often cold; "cold feet" is an expression based on the same physiologic pattern. For people troubled with excessively cold hands and feet, temperature training alone may be indicated. Some migraine sufferers report that their hands get cold just before the headache starts, so learning to raise the hand temperature can help them abort the headache. Temperature training is often used in addition to EMG training for people with problems arising from muscle tension and with general emotional hyper-arousal.

10   Other biofeedback instruments measure other physiological changes. The Galvanic Skin Response or GSR measures changes in sweat gland activity and is the best-known instrument in lie-detector testing. The EEG monitors brain-wave activity, and other instruments monitor heart rate and blood pressure. . . .

11   The majority of biofeedback patients seek this therapy because they have ailments resulting from prolonged stress. When our ancestors had to fight for their lives or flee, those who had responsive bodies

were more likely to survive. Today, when the dangers we face are usually threats to our emotional well-being, we still respond with the same physiological changes. This pattern, called the "fight or flight response," produces changes in our hormone balance and affects a cluster of body processes including heart rate, digestive system activity, blood pressure, and breathing pattern.

12   The stress we face today is less likely to be a brief, focal situation; the stress and its physiological effects may continue for days or months — far beyond what our bodies can tolerate and still remain healthy. We may not be aware of the destructive effects of long-term stress on our bodies until we develop a stress-related ailment, perhaps colitis in one person and high blood pressure in another. It seems likely that inherited predispositions play a part in determining what symptoms we develop from prolonged stress.

13   It is possible to learn a pattern of response that counteracts the debilitating effects of stress on our bodies. This has been named the "relaxation response" by Herbert Benson, M.D., who has used his Harvard laboratory to investigate it. He finds that the relaxation response is evoked by a cluster of techniques with which we all have some familiarity, such as deep relaxation, meditation, and certain yoga practices.

14   Dr. Benson lists four requirements that all techniques for relaxation have in common: (1) a quiet place, (2) a comfortable position, (3) a passive attitude, and (4) the repetition of a peaceful word or phrase to reduce the chatter of the mind. Dr. Benson recommends practicing the relaxation response for one or more ten- or twenty-minute periods every day to counter the effects of unavoidable stress.

15   Biofeedback could be considered an alternative path to achieving the relaxation response for people who have not succeeded in other methods. People who have lost touch with the subtle signals from the part of their bodies most affected by stress can re-learn these signals as they find out how to control the auditory or visual feedback from the instruments monitoring their bodies. With further practice, they learn how to produce the same state without the instruments.

16   After learning to relax the muscles producing the symptom, it is usually easy to learn to enter a state of deep relaxation which is a natural antidote to the fight or flight response with its attendant ills. At the conclusion of therapy people continue the benefits of deep relaxation by some form of daily practice, which may be a routine of tensing and relaxing certain groups of muscles, imagining a flow of warmth progressing up the body from the toes, meditation, or some other relaxation technique.

17   While biofeedback can give a person voluntary control over a distressing symptom like a headache, and deep relaxation can counter the effects of stress on the body as a whole, psychotherapy can augment the treatment by focusing on how the person came to be under so much stress and what alternatives exist to reduce the stress.

18   A woman may find that she achieves success in her career but is
disabled by headaches that vanish when she recognizes that she has
ignored her need to be nurtured. Another woman may discover that a
muscle spasm in her shoulder ceases to trouble her when she realizes
how angry she is at her husband's expectations of her. Biofeedback
plus psychotherapy can be a powerful pair of techniques giving the
patient and the therapist the flexibility to move between the two as
needed.

19   In some clinical practices, biofeedback is administered by a
trained clinician under the supervision of a psychologist or medical
doctor. In other practices, all therapy is administered by a psychologist. The advantage of using a trained biofeedback clinician is financial: a clinician's time is less costly than that of a doctoral-level psychologist. The advantage of having a psychologist conduct the therapy
is that he or she is able to treat not only the ailment but also the person
whose life style and pattern of thinking resulted in the symptom. If a
patient has some difficulty learning voluntary control of the symptom
from the biofeedback instrument, the psychologist can help the person
to work through what is blocking the therapy.

Comprehension

1. According to the reading, what is biofeedback? What does it do? What can't
    it do? What did people expect from it when it first became popular?

2. How is biofeedback administered?

3. What are the four types of biofeedback equipment? How do they work?

4. How are the following terms related to biofeedback: cold feet, fight or flight
    response, relaxation response?

5. What four elements do relaxation techniques require? Give a specific ex-
    ample for each.

Discussion

1. Biofeedback may lead to relaxation for people affected by stress. How
    would you describe stress?

2. What are some things that create stress for you? How do you usually re-
    spond to stress?

3. How do you relax when you are under stress?

Language Practice

Fill in the blanks in the paragraph below with appropriate words from this list. You may use a word more than once.

increases   vessels   voluntary
reduced   muscles   involuntary
flow

Our blood _____ are surrounded by tiny _____ . If they

are contracted, the blood _____ to that organ or part of the body is

_____ ; if they are relaxed, the blood flow _____ . The tension

in these tiny _____ is not usually under _____ control. But

temperature training with biofeedback can give a person _____ control

of this normally _____ function.

Match the terms in Column A with the correct definitions or explanations in Column B. Write the appropriate number in the blanks.

A	**B**
1. biofeedback	_____ heart rate, digestive system activity, blood pressure, breathing pattern
2. biofeedback plus psychotherapy	_____ a form of teaching
3. a cluster of body processes	_____ headaches, high blood pressure, jaw clenching, muscle spasms
4. stress-reducing techniques	_____ deep relaxation, meditation, and certain yoga practices
5. stress-related ailments	_____ a powerful pair of techniques to decrease stress

Choose the appropriate form of the word in each set and write it in the blanks below.

1. tense   tension

Biofeedback can measure muscle _____ . When a patient becomes worried, his/her muscles become _____ . In other words, a person's

muscles _____ in times of stress.

2. contract contraction contracted

Blood vessels are surrounded by small muscles. When an individual is under certain stresses, these muscles _____ and the blood flow decreases. This _____ stops blood from reaching an organ like the brain or stomach. As soon as the individual relaxes, the _____ blood vessels open up again and normal blood flow resumes.

3. responsive respond

How does your body _____ in an emergency? Does it react slowly, or is it _____ to any type of threat?

4. tolerate tolerable intolerable

Our bodies can _____ a certain amount of pain and discomfort. A slight headache, for example, is _____ . However, when the pain is prolonged, then the situation becomes _____ and we have to seek medical assistance.

Read the following definitions. Then fill in the blanks with an appropriate word from the reading.

1. a product that is used for connecting/attaching one item to another (See paragraph 5.) _____

2. a person, especially one living a long time ago, to whom you are related (See paragraph 11.) _____

3. a medicine or an action to protect your body from harmful effects (See paragraphs 3, 11, 16.) _____

4. a news story title usually printed in large letters above the story (See paragraph 1.)   _____

5. a severe and repeated headache (See paragraph 9.)   _____

6. a device that informs you about the activity of the thing to which it is connected (See paragraph 2.)   _____

7. an elastic piece of material in the body that helps parts of the body to move (See paragraph 3.)   _____

8. a loss of feeling and control of body muscles (See paragraph 6.)   _____

9. the natural outer covering of an animal or human body (See paragraph 5.)   _____

10. a liquid that comes out the body through the skin to cool it (See paragraph 10.)   _____

11. an outward sign that may indicate a change in body or mind, possibly because of a disease or disorder (See paragraph 2.)   _____

Choose five of the words from the blanks above and write sentences in which you explain how they are used in connection with biofeedback.

1. _____

2. _____

3. _____

4. _____

5. _____

For each of the following verbs, first write its definition, and then write sentences using it that answer the questions on the left, as in the example below.

rescue   fluctuate   fasten   monitor

EXAMPLE: flee

Definition: *to run away*
              to escape

Who? What?	*People who are in trouble flee.*
	Animals flee from danger.
Where?	*Animals flee to a safe place.*
	Refugees flee from one country to
	another. Criminals flee from prison.
When?	*Children flee when they're afraid.*
	Some criminals flee at night.
Why?	*Some people flee because they're not*
	happy. In the 1920s, immigrants fled
	Europe to find a better place to live.

WORD: rescue

Definition:	_____
Who? What?	_____
	_____
Where?	_____
	_____
When?	_____
	_____
Why?	_____
	_____

Do the other words on another piece of paper.

Fill in the blanks below with appropriate words from this list:

Nouns	Verbs	Adjectives
ailments	counteracts	debilitating
relaxation	feed	routine
threats	monitor	sensitive
well-being	seek	slight

1. It is possible to learn a pattern of response that _____ the _____

   _____ effects of stress on our bodies.

2. At the conclusion of therapy people continue the benefits of deep _____

   _____ by some form of daily practice, which may be a _____

   tensing and relaxing of certain groups of muscles.

3. The majority of biofeedback patients _____ this therapy because

   they have _____ resulting from prolonged stress.

4. Today, when the dangers we face are usually _____ to our emo-

   tional _____ , we respond with the "fight or flight response."

5. The temperature trainer is _____ to temperature changes of hun-

   dredths of a degree, so the patient can become aware of extremely

   _____ changes in finger temperature.

6. There are several types of biofeedback equipment, all of which _____

   body signals and _____ information about extremely small changes

   in body functioning back to the patient.

   Everybody needs to relax. On the lines below, briefly describe one way in
which you relax.

   _____

   _____

_____

_____

_____

Follow-up Activities

1. List five jobs that create severe stress. Compare your list with those of other students. Be prepared to support your choices.

2. During the past week, what were the three most stressful situations for you? Compare your list with those of other students. Also find out how other students reacted to their stressful situations.

3. Find information in the library about the lie-detector test (GSR). Who uses it? Look for an article that discusses the validity of these tests.

4. Look up the words *yoga, yogi,* and *mantra.* Write a brief report describing how the ideas suggested by these words are related to biofeedback.

5. How many words can you make from the letters in the word *biofeedback?* List them below and compare your list with those of other students.

EXAMPLES: bad   back

_____   _____   _____   _____

_____   _____   _____   _____

6. Make the word *tone,* a sound, into a different word by reading the definition and changing *one* letter at a time until you get a new word.

   T O N E =   a sound

   __ __ __ __   a hard part of the body, which could be broken

   __ __ __ __   make someone uninterested

   __ __ __ __   the first thing that happens to a baby

   __ __ __ __   what a match can do

Now write your own definitions for the following word changes. You can change only *one* letter at a time and each time you change a letter, the new word must mean something. Write a definition for each new word.

Change TINY to RUDE.

T I N Y = _____

— — — —   _____

— — — —   _____

— — — —   _____

— — — —   _____

Change FLOW to CRAM.

F L O W = _____

— — — —   _____

— — — —   _____

— — — —   _____

— — — —   _____

Compare your definitions with those of other students.

Chapter Review

Study the information in this chapter's readings. Prepare a list of suggestions about staying healthy. Prepare one list for a young person and another for an elderly person.

Coping

5

In the contemporary world, people move frequently and easily, from one city to another, from one country to another, from the countryside to the city, and so forth. When they come to a new place they often have to adapt to a new way of life. The readings here describe different ways of life and how people adapt to them.

City of Stress

Before You Read

Gordon Mott, a journalist, wrote this article for the *Dallas Times-Herald* about the problems caused by Mexico City's rapidly growing population.

Think About It

If you recently have lived in or visited a large city, have you noticed any problems related to its size?

Is it difficult for you to get around in the city or town where you live? Why or why not?

City of Stress

Gordon D. Mott

1 The past 30 years of growth in Mexico City have meant the disappearance of a lifestyle reminiscent of colonial times — lunch at home, a long siesta and the quiet city home that used to be close to downtown.

2 Now, just to find land to build on, many aspiring homeowners have sought plots in suburban areas. Although the communities aren't far from Mexico City, poor roads force people into long commutes.

3 Oscar Gonzalo Chiquillo, a lawyer in a small law firm, said he leaves home at 6 A.M. from his small two-bedroom house in a middle-class suburb in the State of Mexico, about 15 miles north of the Federal District. He gets to work shortly before 7 A.M.

4 "If I left at 7 o'clock, I wouldn't get into the office until 9:30," he said. "Likewise, I don't leave work until about 9 o'clock and I get home about 10 o'clock. If I leave work at 7, I don't get home until 9:30 anyway."

5 The city's size has forever altered lunch habits. Nearly every businessman or bureaucrat used to go home for lunch, have a siesta and finally return to work between 5 P.M. and 6 P.M.

6 "I can't take the time to go home now," said Javier Caraveo, the city's planning chief. "It takes just an hour to get home and an hour to get back. There wouldn't be any time except to sit down, eat, and get back into the car."

7 Alejandra Moreno, a city historian, also complained that the city's size has determined one's social relationships. "It's so hard to get around that you end up making friends with people who live in your part of town."

8 Jose Ignacio Amor, an architect for the Urban Planning Center of the Valley of Mexico, said his whole life revolves around the southern part of the city.

9 "I haven't been downtown in three months," the young architect said from his large office on the city's southern edge. "I go to movies and restaurants down here. I do all my shopping down here. There's no reason to go anywhere else."

10 Maria Eugenia Negrete, another urban researcher, said: "I don't even have boyfriends in the northern part of the city. It's just not worth it to spend so much time on the Periferico."

11 The Periferico, the only major north-south artery on the western edge of the city, constitutes the bane of nearly everyone who is forced to crawl onto its six narrow lanes. It's a two-hour commuter's nightmare just to reach the largest bedroom communities on the city's northern and southern outskirts.

12 The 10-year-old expressway is a maelstrom of honking horns, lumbering trucks and buses spouting exhaust fumes. More often than not, the lanes are filled with bumper-to-bumper, stop-and-go traffic. Since

there are no breakdown lanes, one overheated car can stall traffic for miles.

13   "My dentist claims that the Periferico is his best source of revenue," said Humberto Munoz, an urban economic researcher. "He says everyone that drives on the Periferico grinds their teeth so much, they need him."

Comprehension

Expand your understanding of the article's main ideas.

1. Why did people in Mexico City want to live in surburban areas?

2. What is happening to the siesta habit? Why?

3. In what ways does living in Mexico City seem to limit people's social life? Give examples.

4. What kinds of problems do Mexico City's commuters have?

5. What other problems are affecting the people who live in Mexico City?

Applications

Relate the article to events in your own life.

1. Why do so many people want to live in large cities?

2. What are the advantages and disadvantages of living in a suburb? In the center of a city?

3. How do the people's life styles described here compare with yours?

4. Describe a trip you took to a large city. How old were you? How did you travel? Where did you stay? Why did you go? What did you like and dislike about the city?

Five Dog Night

Before You Read

John Hanson Mitchell is editor of *Sanctuary*, the Massachusetts Audubon Society magazine that publishes articles about nature and the relationship between people and their natural environment. In this article Mitchell describes an old man who lives in a very cold rural area of the United States.

Think About It

How do people keep their houses warm in cold climates?

Have you ever visited a very cold place? What did you do to stay warm?

Five Dog Night

John Hanson Mitchell

1   Richard Porter of East Charleston, Vermont, aged 75 or 80, does not own an electric blanket. He does not have central heat in his three-room cabin, has not heard of modern airtight wood stoves, does not own a kerosene or gas space heater, and regularly allows the fire in his box-type wood stove to burn itself out each night around eleven o'clock. He is not averse to cold drafts and for this reason has never insulated the pine board walls of his cabin even though the temperatures in East Charleston commonly dip below zero degrees Fahrenheit for weeks at a time. And yet, in spite of his apparent lack of conveniences, Porter says he is never cold at night. He has devised a system of living blankets which automatically pile themselves on his bed in response to the temperature.

2   Porter is the type of mildly eccentric individual who can be found living beyond the confines of the rural towns throughout most of North America. He lives by his wits, working for local logging crews whenever he needs money, picking over the local dump for resources he feels need recycling, and getting through the New England winter with as little expenditure of money and energy as possible. Like many who have deserted human society, Porter keeps a number of dogs for companions. Townspeople regularly see him walking along back roads surrounded by his pack, a mixed crew of all sizes and shapes, some large, some small, some friendly, and the rest too lazy to be unfriendly. Because of his companions he has earned for himself the title "The Dog King" among the townspeople. Not surprisingly, it is his subjects who keep him warm at night.

3   Each winter night about the time the box stove begins to cool, the first of Porter's alternative heating systems — a black and tan hound named Spike — begins to stir from his spot beneath the stove. Spike will climb onto Porter's bed when the room temperature reaches 50 degrees. Louise will get up around 40 degrees. Any colder and the others begin to come in through a dog door which Porter has cut in one of his door panels.

4   Spike and Louise, his favorites, spend most of their time in the cabin. The others come in only to sleep, and only when it's cold. They come in a progression, Porter says. Jeff, a collie-like dog with a thick coat, will move in on those nights when the outside temperature

reaches ten degrees and will join the others on the bed shortly there-
after. Alice, a medium-sized dog of indetermined parentage, arrives
after the temperature dips below ten. But those nights when the mer-
cury dips below zero mark the arrival of the warmest dog of all, an
immense golden-eyed thing named Bull who has a strong shot of Irish
wolfhound in his blood.

5   Porter says that Bull does not normally appreciate such bourgeois
comforts as warm stoves and human companionship. But in his aloof,
dog-like way, he is as devoted to Porter as any dog of his type could
be. Porter believes that it is generally below Bull to come in at night,
let alone climb up on the bed with the lesser beings in the pack. But
zero degree nights get the better of his pride and invariably he deserts
his usual hideout beneath the porch stairs and squeezes in through the
narrow door panel. With Bull on the bed, there is not a night that
Porter cannot endure.

6   Richard Porter has fallen behind the times in some areas of study.
He was not aware of the fact that this country experienced what was
once termed an "energy crisis." On the other hand, he has not been
cold at night for some 65 years in spite of the fact that he lives in one
of the coldest regions in New England and spends no more than one
or two hundred dollars a year on energy — mostly for dog food.

Comprehension

1. How does Porter get money when he needs it?

2. What is his "alternative heating system"?

3. What does the article's title mean?

4. Porter lives in a cold climate. What things does he not have which we might
    expect him to have?

5. What do we learn about Bull's habits?

6. Do we know why Spike and Louise are Porter's favorite dogs?

7. Do we learn why Porter lives the ways he does?

8. In what ways is Porter "behind the times"?

Discussion

1. Do you know any people who live outside their society? If so, do you know
    why they do it?

2. What are some ways to keep cool in a hot climate?

3. In what ways has the "energy crisis" affected your country?

Language Practice

For each of the sentences or parts of sentences underlined below, choose the correct equivalent from the list on the right. Circle your answers.

1. He is not averse to cold drafts.

   a. He doesn't mind

   b. He doesn't get

   c. He is bothered by

2. There is not a night that Porter cannot endure.

   a. Porter can stand any night.

   b. Porter can survive most of the night.

   c. Porter can't be comfortable at night.

3. Porter has fallen behind the times.

   a. has trouble walking around.

   b. does not have a clock.

   c. is out of touch with events.

4. He spends no more than one or two hundred dollars a year on energy.

   a. It probably costs him at least $200 a year.

   b. It probably costs him less than $200 a year.

   c. It probably costs him more than $200 a year.

With which of the situations in the right-hand column can you associate the sentences below? Circle your answers.

1. Any colder and the others begin to come in.

   a. It's not cold so the others stay out.

   b. If it gets colder, the others come in.

   c. Any one of the others that gets cold comes in.

2. He lives by his wits.

   a. He lives with somebody.

   b. He lives by doing things in cooperation with others.

   c. He lives by taking advantage of opportunities.

3. It is generally <u>below</u> Bull to come in at night.

    a. Bull is usually too proud to come in at night.

    b. Bull comes in at night and sleeps under the bed.

    c. When Bull comes in at night, he sleeps on top of another dog.

4. It is generally below Bull to come in at night, <u>let alone</u> climb up on the bed.

    a. Bull likes to be alone on the bed.

    b. Bull needs help in climbing up on the bed.

    c. Bull doesn't usually get on the bed.

Fill in the blanks below with an appropriate word or phrase from the left-hand column above.

1. _____ and my nose will become an icicle.

2. When the temperature dips below zero degrees Fahrenheit, it is difficult to breathe, _____ run for a mile.

3. The young man had very little income and had to survive _____ .

4. She's a proud cat; she feels that it is _____ her to ask for food.

Make sure you know the meaning of the words listed below. Then fill in the blanks in the sentences with a word from the list. You do not have to use all of the words, and you may use a word more than once.

        regularly   invariably   automatically   never

1. I _____ have fruit juice when I get up in the morning.

2. I _____ put on a seat belt when I enter a car.

3. I _____ close my eyes when I sneeze.

4. I _____ swallow when I eat or drink.

5. I _____ breathe when I am underwater.

Fill in the blanks in the paragraph below with appropriate words from this list:

lack	desert	get through	companions
devise	dip	conveniences	appreciate
system	comforts	spend	

If we move to a rural area of northern New England and can live with as

few _____ as possible, we may live with a _____ of many

_____ . Life may become a progression of problems and we will

_____ our time trying to _____ ways of _____ the

days. When the temperature _____ below zero, we will _____

the warmth of a wood stove. If we feel lonely, we will look for _____.

If things get too bad, we can _____ the cold north and go south.

Read this paragraph:

In spite of . . . (something) or despite . . . (something) means not to be affected by that thing or prevented from doing something by that thing. For example: "In spite of the cold, I took off my coat and ran through the snow."

From the set of phrases below, choose the one that is equivalent to the underlined part of the following sentence.

In spite of his apparent lack of conveniences, Porter says he is never cold at night.

1. _____ Since he has enough conveniences, . . .

2. _____ In case he seems not to have conveniences, . . .

3. _____ Although he does not seem to have conveniences, . . .

Read the following sentences, which are similar in meaning.

Despite the heat, she ran for two miles.	Although it was hot, she ran for two miles.
In spite of having five blankets, he felt cold.	Although he had five blankets, he felt cold.

On the lines below, rewrite each sentence using the preceding sentences as a model. Use *although*.

1. In spite of her interest in the city, she moved to a rural area.

   _____

   _____

2. Despite his not having any central heat, Richard keeps warm in the winter.

   _____

   _____

On the lines below, combine a phrase from Column A with a phrase from Column B, using *despite* or *in spite of* to connect the two.

A	**B**
John's living in a cold climate	she walks two miles a day
her age	he couldn't earn enough to buy a car
his efforts	he doesn't spend much on energy
my having three dogs	I'm still cold in the winter

1. _____

2. _____

3. _____

4. _____

Complete the following sentences in your own words.

1. Despite her lack of money, _____ .

2. In spite of having a thick coat, _____ .

3. _____ , Porter keeps warm at night.

4. _____ , he does not own an electric blanket.

The following sentences are not in correct order. Rewrite them in the correct order on the lines below.

When it dips below ten degrees, Alice arrives.
He comes in when the temperature drops below zero.
Spike and Louise are already there because they spend most of their time in the cabin.
The last dog to enter is Bull.
The dogs enter the cabin in a progression.
Jeff comes in when the temperature reaches ten degrees.
The others come in when it's cold.

_____

_____

_____

_____

_____

_____

Retell a part of the reading by using the key words below to make sentences in the blanks.

Porter   dogs   companions

_____

walks   roads   pack of dogs

_____

large   small

_____

friendly   unfriendly

_____

title   "Dog King"

_____

Retell a part of the reading by answering the following questions. Combine your answers into good sentences.

How old is Porter?   _____

Where does he live?   _____

What does he have in his cabin?   _____

Is he cold at night?   _____

How does he keep himself   _____
warm?

Make a story by choosing one sentence from each of the following sets and writing your sentences on the lines below. Add connectives such as *and, but,* or *also* between sentences when it is appropriate.

1. a. Mary Ferrari is 27 years old.
   b. Catherine Fitzgerald is 72 years old.
   c. Lisa Feldman is 19 years old.

2. a. She lives in Manhattan.
   b. She lives in Miami.
   c. She lives in northern Montana.

3. a. Her apartment is large but she does not have many conveniences.
   b. Her apartment is small but she does not lack any conveniences.
   c. Her apartment is medium-sized but she does not have any heat.

4. a. She gets a good income from her parents.
   b. She lives by her wits.
   c. She works for a local stove manufacturer.

5. a. But she does not like to spend any money.
   b. But she likes to spend all her money.
   c. But she doesn't get very much money.

6. a. In the evening you can see her in department stores.
   b. In the evening you can see her picking over the local dump.
   c. In the evening you can see her near her stove at home.

_____

_____

_____

_____

_____

_____

_____

Complete the following paragraph in your own words.

Some people like to have dogs because _____

_____

_____ .

Others don't like to keep dogs because _____

_____ .

Follow-up Activities

1. Pretend that you are interviewing Richard Porter. What answers do you think he would give to the following questions?

   How old are you?

   Do you live here alone?

   How is this cabin heated?

   Why do you have so many dogs?

   Why did you come to live here?

   What do you think about the present condition of the world?

   Do you mind being interviewed?

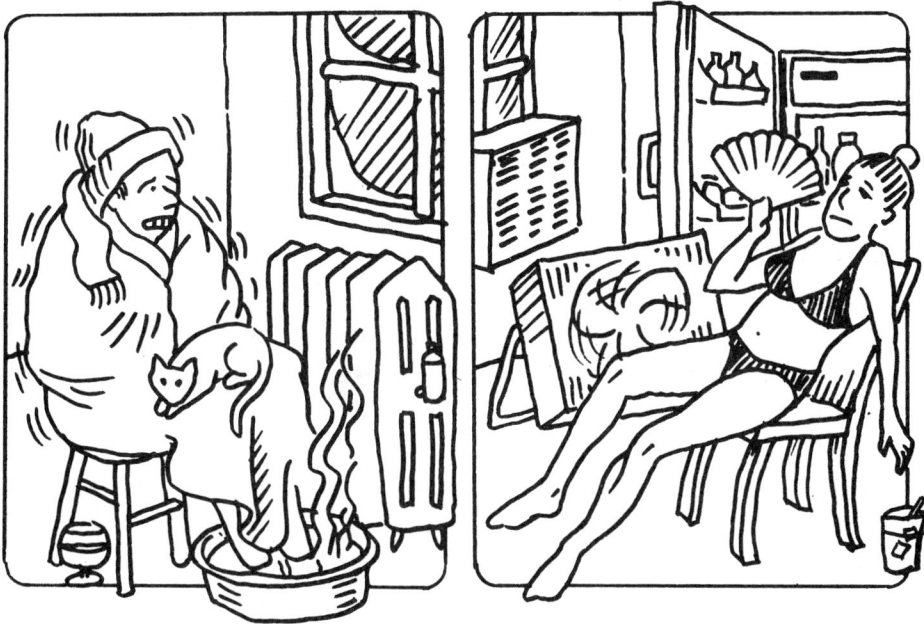

2. Describe the problems of the people in the above drawings. How are they coping with their environments?

3. Find out how people who live in hot climates keep cool. List as many ways of keeping cool as possible (consider types of buildings, machines, clothes, activities, and so on).

4. Find out how people who live in cold climates keep warm. List as many ways as possible (consider types of buildings, machines, clothes, activities, and so on).

5. If you are in a country where pets are common, interview five people to find out if they have pets in their homes. If they do, ask them what kind of pets they have, why they have pets, what they feed them, and how important the pets are to them. If they do not have pets, ask them why. Compare your results with those of other students.

Topics for Further Discussion or Writing

1. People may desert society in different ways. Some, like hermits, go to live in isolated areas; others live their own lives in crowded areas. Have you known any people who live very differently from those around them?

2. If you could live anywhere in the world, where would you live?

3. If you could live at any time (with the help of a time machine), what time (past, present, or future) would you choose and why?

4. Porter talks about the comforts of life, such as a warm stove and companionship. What is essential and what is a comfort? What are the minimum essentials that every family should have?

The Bakhtiari: Nomads

Before You Read

J. Bronowski, an anthropologist, wrote a book about the development of human beings called *The Ascent of Man*. In this selection, he describes the life of the Bakhtiari people and the challenges they face as they migrate from place to place.

Think About It

Do you know of any groups of people who are always migrating?

When you travel, what do you take with you to make yourself feel "at home"?

The Bakhtiari: Nomads

J. Bronowski

1 There are some nomad tribes who still go from one grazing ground to another: the Bakhtiari in Iran, for example. As with other nomadic herdsmen, their herds are all-important. Before 10,000 B.C., nomads used to follow the natural migration of wild animals. But sheep and goats have no natural migrations. They were first domesticated about ten thousand years ago. And when they were domesticated, the nomads took on the responsibility of nature; they had to lead the helpless herd.

2 While the men lead the animals, the role of women in nomad tribes is to produce children, especially boys. Apart from that, their duties lie in preparing food and clothes. Like the men, the lives of the women center on the herd. They milk the animals and they make yoghourt from the milk. They have only the simple technology that can be carried on daily journeys from place to place. The simplicity is not romantic; it is a matter of survival. Everything must be light enough to be carried, to be set up every evening and to be packed away again every morning. When the women spin wool with their simple, ancient

devices, it is for immediate use, to make the repairs that are essential on the journey — no more.

3   It is not possible in the nomad life to make things that will not be needed for several weeks. They could not be carried. *And* in fact the Bakhtiari do not know how to make them. If they need metal pots, they barter them from settled people or from gipsy workers who specialize in metals. A nail, a toy or a child's bell is something that is traded from outside the tribe. The Bakhtiari life is too narrow to have time or skill for specialization. There is no room for innovation, because there is not time, on the move, between evening and morning, coming and going all their lives, to develop a new device or a new thought. The only habits that survive are the old habits. The only ambition of the son is to be like the father.

4   Every night is the end of a day like the last, and every morning will be the beginning of a journey like the day before. When the day breaks, there is one question in everyone's mind: Can the herd get over the next high pass? One day on the journey, the highest pass of all must be crossed. This is the pass Zadeku, twelve thousand feet high on the Zagros. For the tribe must move on, the herdsmen must find new pastures every day, because at these heights grazing is exhausted in a single day.

5   Every year the Bakhtiari cross six ranges of mountains on the outward journey (and cross them again to come back). They march through snow and the spring flood water. *And* in only one respect has their life advanced beyond that of ten thousand years ago. The nomads of that time had to travel on foot and carry their own packs. The Bakhtiari have pack-animals — horses, donkey, mules — which have only been domesticated since that time. Nothing else in their lives is new. And nothing is memorable. Nomads have no memorials, even to the dead.

6   The spring migration of the Bakhtiari is a heroic adventure; yet, their adventure leads them nowhere. The summer pastures themselves will only be a stopping place. The head of the family has worked seven years to build a herd of fifty sheep and goats. He expects to lose ten of them in the migration if things go well. If they go badly, he may lose twenty out of that fifty. Those are the odds of the nomad life, year in and year out.

7   Who knows, in any one year, whether the old when they have crossed the passes will be able to face the final test: the crossing of the Bazuft River? The tribesmen, the women, the pack animals and the herd are all exhausted. It will take a day to get the herd across the river. But this, here, now is the testing day. Today is the day on which the young become men, because the survival of the herd and the family depends on their strength. For the young man, life for a moment comes alive now. And for the old, it dies. What happens to the old when they cannot cross the last river? Nothing. They stay behind to die. They accept the nomad custom; they come to the end of their journey, and there is no place at the end.

Comprehension

1. In what ways is the life of the Bakhtiari centered on their animals?

2. Why do they have to travel so much?

3. How is work divided between men and women?

4. What is the "final test"?

5. The author suggests that the Bakhtiari have not been innovative because their lives are so busy. Do you think that is a convincing reason?

Discussion

1. What is the division of labor in your family? What do the men do? The women? The children?

2. The Bakhtiari way of life represents an early stage in the economic development of human beings. What do you think the next stage was?

3. Do you think nomadic life still exists today in many places? If not, why is it disappearing?

Language Practice

Find the meaning of the underlined words below. Then rewrite each sentence, substituting appropriate words or phrases for the underlined ones.

1. The nomads took on the responsibility of nature.

_____

2. When the women spin their wool with their simple, ancient devices, it is for immediate use.

_____

3. And in only one respect has their life advanced beyond that of ten thousand years ago.

_____

4. The tribesmen, the women, the pack animals and the herd are all ex-hausted.

_____

5. They come to the end of their journey.

_____

Choose the appropriate forms of the words in each of the following sets, and write them in the blanks below.

1. simple   simply   simplicity

The _____ of Bakhtiari technology is a result of their nomadic life.

Their tools are _____ and they live _____ because they have to

carry everything with them.

2. responsible   responsibly   responsibility

In the city the men were _____ for building houses while the prep-

aration of food was the _____ of the women. Children acted

_____ if they helped their parents.

3. innovate   innovative   innovatively   innovation

Bronowski feels that the Bakhtiari are not an _____ society and

their lack of _____ results from their way of life. He seems to suggest

that people who _____ need to be free from a busy routine.

4. survive   surviving   survival

In order for large populations to _____ , village agriculture was

necessary, and the _____ of the village depended on knowledge of crop

planting.

Read each of the following phrases. Then use the lines below to describe a situation in your life or in the life of someone you know that illustrates the meaning of the phrase. Use the phrases in your description.

1. face a test

_____

_____

_____

2. take on responsibility

_____

_____

_____

3. an old habit that has survived

_____

_____

_____

4. a memorable event

_____

_____

_____

WORD LADDER: Change the word *herd* into the word *goat* by changing only one letter at each step on the ladder. The definition on the left will help you know what letter to change. If you have a problem, go on to the next clue and then work backward.

EXAMPLE: 1.   a place to play in back of a house

2.   wool for a sweater

3.   a building for farm animals

HARD
YARD
YARN
BARN

1. Top part of the body

2. Not alive

3. A common word used to begin a letter

4. Be afraid

5. Listen to

6. Make something hot

7. A chair or bench

8. The Mediterranean, Caspian, and Black _____

9. Observes; notices

10. Insects that make honey

11. A red onion-shaped vegetable

12. A yellow alcoholic beverage

13. A panda, polar, brown, or black _____

14. Pull apart; rip

15. A group of people who play a sport

16. A ray of light

17. Hit again and again

18. Ship

HERD
GOAT

Match the items in Column A with those in Column B by writing the number next to the associated term. One example has been filled in for you.

A

1. Bakhtiari
2. boy's ambition
3. boys become men
4. cross
5. every day and night
6. herds
7. journey
8. milk product
9. new ideas
10. nomads' goal
11. pack and carry
12. pots, knives, and so on
13. 10,000 years ago
14. wool

B

_____ Bakhtiari's main concern

_____ domesticated sheep and goats

_____ find new pastures

_____ be like his father

_____ leads them nowhere

_____ no time

_____ only essential items

_____ six mountain ranges

_____ identical

_____ the testing day

_____ traded from outside the tribe

___*1*___ tribe

_____ used for repairs

_____ yoghourt

On the following lines, write a sentence using the information in each matched pair above. Be sure to add any necessary words to make your sentences grammatically correct.

EXAMPLE: 1. *The Bakhtiari are a tribe of nomads.*

2. _____

3. _____

4. _____

5. _____

6. _____

7. _____

8. _____

9. _____

10. _____

11. _____

12. _____

13. _____

14. _____

The author describes the roles of men and, especially, of women in Bakhtiari society. The duties of the women include milking the animals and preparing the food, for example. Refer to a family that you know and on the lines below list the duties of the family members (mother, father, children, other relatives if they live with the family). For example: setting the table

Father	**Mother**
_____	_____
_____	_____
_____	_____
_____	_____

Brother	**Sister**
_____	_____
_____	_____

Other	
_____	_____
_____	_____

Follow-up Activities

1. Collect some information about other nomad groups from reference books or magazines. For example, see the *Science Digest* (January 1983) for an article on the Bedouins, or the *Unesco Courier* (June 1983) for "The New Nomads."

2. When people pack for a trip, they have to decide what they will need. Choose two kinds of trips (for example, a trip to another country for two months; a trip to the mountains for a week) and list the most important things to take. Compare your lists with those of other students.

3. Pretend that you have to live alone on a desert island. If you could take only five things with you, what would they be? Compare your list with those of other students.

4. If you could take one record or tape to the island (it has a little electricity), and one book, which would you take? Why? Survey the class.

America's Newest Immigrants

Before You Read

This article, published in *Redbook Magazine*, describes the difficulties that refugees from Southeast Asia face as they try to adjust to new technologies and a new culture in the United States.

Think About It

What kinds of adjustment problems have you experienced when living in a new place?

How would you feel about living in a new place if you knew that you could never go back to your country?

America's Newest Immigrants

Claire Safran

1   Imagine that you have been set down in a strange land, on an unknown street. The people around you have skin of a different color, eyes of a different shape. They speak a language that is foreign to you.

Imagine too that you are not here as a tourist for a brief, exotic visit. The door to this alien new world has opened to you and the door to your beloved old world is tightly closed, perhaps forever.

2   For the 340,000 Indochinese who have fled to the United States in recent years, this is reality, not imagination. Many have come not only across thousands of miles of space but also through a warp in time. Some are amazed by a small handle that produces a flow of water, by a little switch that brings light to a darkened room, by another light that goes on inside the cold box where food is kept. Can openers, vacuum cleaners, toasters, steam irons — all are foreign to them.

3   For others, the technology is less strange than the culture, the values, the everyday habits. They are puzzled by the American dating game, by the divorce rate, by the ordinary sound of a wife's disagreeing with her husband. Arriving here from a country where schoolteachers are revered, a Vietnamese mother does not know what to make of the critical talk at a PTA meeting. Coming from a country where a physical touch is a deep intimacy, they are uncomfortable with handshakes. When a well-meaning schoolteacher puts her arm around the shoulders of a young Cambodian student to encourage and praise her, the child feels something close to panic.

4   Who are these people?

5   They are the boat people. They came — and are still coming — out of Vietnam on fragile, aging fishing boats. They are remnants of war and hunger in Cambodia. They are survivors of an invaded Laos.

6   These human beings have become the chief export of their native countries. The luckier ones arrived in 1975, fleeing after the collapse of South Vietnam. Most have arrived more recently. Nobody knows how many have fled Vietnam, Cambodia and Laos. Nobody knows how many have died while trying. Hundreds of thousands have been given a haven by various nations. More hundreds of thousands still huddle in refugee camps in Thailand, Hong Kong, Malaysia. Each month there's an agony of selection: Who is most deserving, because of past service to this country? Who is most closely related to someone already here? Who is most likely to make it in an alien land? Then an additional 14,000 — mostly adults in their 20s and 30s and young children — are flown to the United States.

7   And what then?

8 Her name is a musical note. Do Thi Minh Ngoc (with a silent g). She is 30 years old, a nurse in a home for the aged in San Antonio, Texas. "I am different. I am" — she searches for the right word — "a minority. Some people look at me funny on the street." When she arrived, in December of 1978, she was euphoric, dizzy, with the simple pleasure of being safe. "When I came to America before, I was impressed by how rich you are," she says. "Now I am impressed by how free you are. You allow me to be a human being here." As the months passed,

the sadness, the sense of loss, pressed in. "I am a small boat on a great sea." In San Antonio, Ngoc was reunited with her widowed mother and six brothers and sisters, some of them married with children. "We try to adapt to your American ways but we stay close," she says. "We do what the parent says." With a smile she adds: "Usually." For Ngoc the family is her identity, her solace, her source of strength. She lives with one sister's family in a house on the edge of the city.

9   One evening, at a family get-together, she reflected, "These happy times — they are when I miss my husband the most." Some customs are different. There are two dining tables, one surrounded by men, the other for women. The hostess stated, "Even when we don't have enough money, we buy clothes for the children. They must not feel ashamed at school." Her husband, a former air force major, talks of working in restaurant kitchens before landing his current job with an aerial surveying company. "I am happy with what I have," he says, "but my children will have more. For them it will be better."

10 Nun Chhoeurn, a 22-year-old Cambodian woman, lives in San Antonio with an uncle and his children, a family of ten. The house they live in has settled askew over the years and badly needs paint. The furniture as well as their clothing is secondhand, donations from a local church. Chhoeurn has moved across space and also time, from a farming village to a modern city. Electricity is new to her; so is indoor plumbing.

11   Unlike Ngoc and her family, who arrived here with work and language skills, Chhoeurn will need more help. The Federal Government spends an estimated $2,800 for each refugee over a period of two years. When she has learned some English, Chhoeurn will go to school to learn the job skill that will make her a taxpayer. It is not a totally free ride; like the other recent refugees, she has signed a promissory note to repay the government for her air fare. "I don't dare to think of studying anything very high," she says. "I am simple. I am a girl from the rice fields." Her view of the United States is basic. "I had so little and now I have so much. Here one must work hard, but here it is easy to eat."

12 When Laos fell to the Communists, the Sengsouvang family fled to Thailand with their three children. They spent more than three years there before coming to California. In the first week, a volunteer member of the International Rescue Committee helped the husband, Somsack, find a job repairing old furniture. "I lost my mother in Laos," says Somsack. "Now Shirley (the volunteer) is my mother."

13   People like Ngoc, Chhoeurn and Somsack are the survivors. They are all young adults in their 20s and 30s — the "best" ages to be a refugee, according to sociologists. Middle-aged and older people may find it too hard to adjust; they may become like the former school principal who now does janitor's work in a Chicago store; when he sees someone he knows coming through the doorway, he rushes to

hide in shame in a back room. Young children and teen-agers may adapt too readily; they may become like the 12-year-old in Bridgeport, Connecticut, a spokesperson for her family, glib in the new language and customs, a stranger to her own traditions. A refugee mother worries, "How will the children remember Cambodia?"

Comprehension

1. Why did the schoolteacher put her arm around the shoulders of the young Cambodian student?

2. What is the most important thing for Ngoc?

3. How are Ngoc and her family different from refugees like Chhoeurn?

4. What age group finds adjustment to a new way of living most difficult?

5. Why is selecting refugees for immigration to the United States so difficult?

6. Is this Ngoc's first time in the United States? Explain your answer.

7. Is Ngoc married or single? Explain your answer.

8. What is the refugees' attitude toward their future in the United States?

9. How do refugee parents feel about their children's adapting to an American way of living?

Discussion

1. Identify some refugee groups in other areas of the world. How are they adapting to their new environments?

2. When someone moves permanently into another culture, what are the most difficult adjustments that a person has to make? Support your answer with an example.

3. Do you think a world culture that would be the same for everyone is possible? Do you think it is desirable?

Language Practice

If you think a statement below is true, put a T in the blank beside it. If you think a statement is false, put an F.

1. _____ 340,000 refugees have left Vietnam.

2. _____ Dating is strange to the refugees.

3. _____ Teachers in Vietnam are not as respected as American teachers.

4. _____ Shaking hands is a common custom in Vietnam.

5. _____ The migration of boat people to the United States has stopped.

6. _____ The exact number of Indochinese refugees is not known.

7. _____ Not every refugee comes to the United States.

8. _____ The majority of refugees to the United States are children and old people.

9. _____ The process of selecting refugees to come to the United States is an easy one.

10. _____ Young children have difficulties adapting to American life.

After you correct the above true or false exercise, reread the false statements. Correct all the false statements by writing the correct information on the lines below.

EXAMPLE: _____F_____ In Vietnam, touching someone is quite ordinary.

Touching someone is not ordinary.

Touching is a sign of deep intimacy.

People don't usually shake hands.

_____

_____

_____

_____

_____

Note these expressions: a get-together
know what to make of
to make it
well-meaning
secondhand

1. Find the expression in the reading.

2. Give your definition of each expression on the lines below.

    a. a get-together: _____

    b. know what to make of: _____

    c. to make it: _____

    d. well-meaning: _____

    e. secondhand: _____

3. Think of another situation in which each of the above expressions could be used and write a sentence using it on the lines below.

    a. _____

    b. _____

    c. _____

    d. _____

    e. _____

Read the following definitions in the left-hand column. Then fill in the blanks with an appropriate word from the reading.

EXAMPLE: a cold box where food is kept   *a refrigerator*

1. a person who travels to a place for pleasure and sightseeing (See paragraph 1.)   _____

2. a part of the body to which one's arms are connected (See paragraph 3.)   _____

3. a machine that cleans floors and furniture by pulling in the dirt (See paragraph 2.)   _____

4. a device that makes bread hot, dry, and brown (See paragraph 2.)   _____

5. an action that people may do when they meet for the first time (See paragraph 3.)   _____

6. a need for food (See paragraph 5.)   _____

7. a product that one country sends out to another country (See paragraph 6.)   _____

8. a person who cares for sick people (See paragraph 8.)   _____

9. a married woman whose husband has died (See paragraph 8.)   _____

10. a person who works without receiving money (See paragraph 12.)   _____

11. a person who lives after a terrible accident or tragedy (See paragraph 13.)   _____

12. a person who takes care of the inside of a building (See paragraph 13.)   _____

13. a device that turns on or shuts off electrical appliances and lights (See paragraph 2.)   _____

14. a person who pays a required amount of money to the government to support national spending (See paragraph 11.)   _____

15. a device that presses clothes to make them flat and smooth (See paragraph 2.)   _____

When people arrive at their destination, they can compare their expectations with what they find.

How were your expectations different from the experiences you had in the place to which you traveled? Were you surprised, disappointed, angry? Why? Answer these questions in your own words on the lines below.

_____

_____

_____

_____

_____

_____

For each of the following words, write its definition, and then write sentences using it and answering the questions, as in the example below.

adapt   donate   rush   search   stare

EXAMPLE: flee

Definition: *to run away*
to escape

Who? What: *People who are in trouble flee.*
Animals flee from danger.

Where? *Animals flee to a safe place.*
Refugees flee from one country to another. Criminals flee from prison.

When? *Children flee when they're afraid.*
Some criminals flee at night.

Why? *Some people flee because they're not happy. In the 1920s, immigrants fled Europe to find a better place to live.*

WORD: adapt

Definition: _____

Who? What? _____

Where? _____

When? _____

Why?   _____

                          _____

Do the other words on another piece of paper.

When people travel to another city or country, they usually have expectations of what that place is going to be like. Their expectations may be based on what they have read or heard about that place.

On the lines below, list some of the expectations you had before you traveled to _____ (a city in your country or a foreign country).

_____

_____

_____

_____

_____

_____

On what were your expectations based?

_____

_____

_____

Follow-up Activities

1. Collect information about a group of refugees. Find out why they became refugees, and how they left their country. Why did they go to the country where they live now? How do they feel about their immigration now? Do they create any problems for the host country?

2. Choose a country that you have visited or are familiar with (that is not your home country).

   a. List five customs of this country that are similar to and five that are different from those of your country.

   b. Write your information in two paragraphs, one giving the similarities and one the differences.

   c. Compare your information with that of other students.

3. Find out about the food habits of someone from another country. Ask these questions:

   When do you eat your meals?
   Which is the largest meal?
   Which meal do you enjoy most? Why?
   What kind of foods do you eat at each meal?
   What foods do you personally dislike the most?
   (You may add questions of your own.)

   Then compare your survey with those of other students.

Chapter Review

1. Compare the environments of "City of Stress" and "Five-Dog Night." Which environment do you think is more difficult to live in? Explain why.

2. What do you think would be the greatest difficulty for the Bakhtiari if they moved to a large city?

3. People often regret their actions. Do you think any of the people mentioned in this chapter might regret their actions? Why?

Relationships

6

The readings in this chapter describe personal experiences. They focus on some of the most important relationships in our lives: between parents and children; friends; men and women; and students and teachers.

Best Friends

Before You Read

In her book *Blooming*, Susan Allen Toth describes growing up in the town of Ames, Iowa. In this selection she writes about friends and her memory of her first "best" friend.

Think About It

When you were in elementary school, did you have a best friend? If you did, is that person still your friend?

Did you ever change from one group of friends to another? Do you remember why you did that?

Best Friends

Susan Allen Toth

1   Girlfriends were as essential as mothers. I could survive weeks, even months, without a boyfriend, although I did need to be able to produce one in those endless circular conversations of "Who do you like best?" "Do you think he likes me or Celia better?" "Don't you agree with us that Herb is a fool?" "Would you ever sit next to Jim if you didn't have to?" But I always had to have a best friend.

2   A set of girlfriends provided a sense of security, as belonging to any group does. But having a best friend was more complicated: using a friend as a mirror or as a model, expanding your own knowledge through someone else's, painfully acquiring social skills. What little we learned about living with another person in an equal relationship, outside our own families, we learned from our girlfriends. It certainly wasn't a full preparation for marriage, but it was the only one some of us ever got.

3   My earliest memory of a best friend is a humiliating one. After spending a year in California in third grade, I returned to Ames to skip a grade and suddenly enter fifth. We had just moved to a new house in a different neighborhood, so I also had to switch to the other elementary school on the campus side of town. Both schools joined at Welch Junior High, where we children remained together, a relatively unchanging group, until we moved downtown to merge with Central Junior High in Ames High School. By then we already had our friends.

4   My year away had erased a lot, and I was a new kid in fifth grade, suspiciously smart and a year too young. I felt lost and lonely, and the only girl who would . . . spend any time with me on the playground or after school was Margie Dwyer. Margie, though rather pretty, was shy and awkward. Her dark hair was twisted in old-fashioned braids on top of her head, emphasizing her sallow skin. I seem to remember she wore one dark plaid jumper all the time. Her father was a janitor somewhere at the college, and they lived in a basement apartment in an old building not far from our house. I don't remember visiting there, or her parents, but I do remember how grateful I was to hold hands with Margie, who smiled at me as we skipped . . . down the sidewalk. But I clearly knew then and remembered with shame later that Margie, like me, . . . had no set of friends, no status. After we stopped being best friends the next year, she became best friends with "Sappy" Strickland, the dumbest girl in class. Years later Margie dropped out of high school and married an older man, an auto mechanic. No one noticed.

5   What humiliates me about my memory of Margie is how quickly I dropped her when, in sixth grade, I was suddenly adopted into an acceptable set of friends. There weren't, in fact, many sets to choose from. With two sections of each grade, about thirty students in each, we had a "pool" of sixty; roughly half of those were boys; so thirty

girls had to divide themselves into appropriate groups. Six formed the elite, a group so tight, so deliberately exclusive, that they earned themselves the name of "the Society Six." They were the prettiest, most sophisticated, and stylish girls and naturally included all the ninth-grade cheerleaders. They chose the boyfriends they wanted from the homeroom presidents, athletes, and other "neat" boys.

Comprehension

Expand your understanding of the story's main ideas.

1. Which were more important for the writer, girlfriends or boyfriends?
2. What did the author feel that she learned from her girlfriends?
3. Why didn't she have any friends when she entered the fifth grade?
4. Why is her memory of Margie a humiliating one?

Applications

Relate the story to events in your own life.

1. How important were friends for you when you were in elementary school? What kinds of things did you do together?
2. How important were friends for you when you were in secondary school? What kinds of things did you do together?
3. Describe your first "best" friend. What did he or she look like? Where did you meet her or him? How long did the friendship last?
4. In what ways do young boys and young girls get together in your country? Do girls in high school have boyfriends? Do high school boys have girlfriends?

His Son, the Artist

Before You Read

Gene Light, a publishing house art director, wrote this article for the *New York Times* about his relationship with his father. His description calls attention to differences between generations and how family members adjust to each other.

Think About It

Have you done anything that surprised your parents? If you did, how did they react?

Do you know many young people who are doing the same work as their parents?

His Son, the Artist

Gene Light

1 Every family has its "in" joke. The standing gag in mine was that my father never quite knew what I did for a living.

2 My father was a butcher. His father, uncles and brothers were butchers. He married the cashier at the butcher shop he worked in. Her brothers were all butchers. When I was born, my mother vowed I could be anything I wanted to be except a butcher.

3 As a youngster, I drew pictures all the time, mostly airplanes like all the other kids. Because of this, my mother decided I should go to art school. Before I knew what was happening, I was taking the test for the High School of Music and Art and then traveling an hour and a half from my home in Brooklyn to the school in upper Manhattan.

4 "My son, the artist," was the way my father introduced me to his customers. I worked in his butcher shop every Saturday all through high school. My father naturally assumed I would take over the store when I graduated. When I announced that I had won a scholarship to the Cooper Union School of Art and wanted to continue my art training, he was stunned. He suddenly realized that I was taking this art thing seriously. According to him, "Butchers, grocers, shoemakers . . . that was a way to make a living. Butchers especially . . . people always had to eat! Artists starved in . . . in . . ."

5 "Garrets, Pop."

6 "Whatever."

7 It was useless for me to explain that I was not going to be a painter but a commercial artist. The nuances of my chosen profession escaped him. An artist was an artist — and they starved.

8 Ten years later, my father sold his butcher shop and retired. I was an art director with *Life* magazine, married with two children and moving into my first house in the suburbs. My father came to see the new house, and I noticed a quizzical look on his face. He simply could not understand how "the artist" managed to feed and clothe his grandchildren.

9 I knew he was terribly proud of me. I heard it all the time from the neighbors on the street in Brooklyn where I grew up. He was always bragging about his son, "the artist who draws for *Life* magazine."

Every week my father would get the magazine, and every week he would call and ask, "What did you draw in the magazine this week?" I'd explain that I didn't draw anything. I designed the pages. I placed the photographs, picked the typefaces. He would mumble to himself. Obviously, I was getting my paycheck under false pretenses and would soon be found out.

10 In December of 1972, *Life* folded. Needless to say, I was upset. I was at home watching the news reports of the magazine's death, when the phone rang. I knew it was my father. Eventually, he came out with it: "If you were a butcher, you wouldn't be out of work now." He tried to say it lightly, but I knew he meant it. I never loved the man more and was actually glad to hear it, for somehow it meant my world was still intact.

11 "Do you still remember how to cut meat?"

12 "Yes, Pop."

13 "Remember, people always have to eat."

14 For the last 12 years, I have been art director for a publishing house. Every month, my father gets in the mail the 20 or so books we publish. He calls to tell me how much he likes my paintings on the covers. I no longer explain that I design the covers, choose and place the type and then commission other people to paint them. I just take the credit and thank him. He has pictures to point to and show the neighbors.

15 The family gag about my father's not knowing what I do for a living hit home sharply a few months ago. My son called from California. He's a talent agent with a major agency in Los Angeles. He had had a great offer from a rival company, and he wanted my advice about changing jobs. I said something about "doing what's best for your career in the future," but I realized I didn't know enough about what he actually does to advise him.

16 I remembered eight years back when he called from college and said he had decided he wanted to go into show business. I mumbled the usual: "It's your life and your decision." But when I hung up, I turned to my wife and said, "Show business? What kind of way is that to make a living?" Why hadn't he chosen medicine or law or engineering? "Or being a butcher," my wife said. "People always have to eat."

17 My son must have made the right decision. At 28, he's obviously successful. When I visited his office for the first time, I was impressed. His secretary kept interrupting, asking if he would take a call from this person or that. She was using names that anyone would immediately recognize. For a moment, I thought the little punk had set me up and that the woman was making up the names to impress me. I caught my son looking at me, and I'm sure I had the same quizzical expression I used to see on my father's face. I suppose that unless a man's children work at exactly what he himself does, a father never quite knows what they really do. The intense love, bordering on the painful, always makes a man slightly scared for his children. How could this kid, who couldn't pick up his own socks, be trusted with whatever the heck it is someone is trusting him with?

18   Someday my son's son will tell him what he is going to do with his life. I know my son will think, "What the hell kind of a way is that to making a living?" He will call me, and I will say, "Tell him to be a butcher. People always have to eat."

19   By the way, my father no longer says, "My son, the artist." He now says, "My grandson, the talent agent." He also subscribes to *Variety.*

Comprehension

1. How did the mother and father of the author differ on what career they wanted for their son?

2. Why didn't Light's father want him to be an artist?

3. What are some things that Light's father didn't understand about Light's profession?

4. How would you describe the relationship between Light and his father? How did they feel about each other?

5. In what ways was Light's relationship with his son different from and similar to his relationship with his father?

6. What does the final paragraph tell us about Light's father?

Discussion

1. Why do parents often have problems with their children when the children are deciding on careers?

2. What are some differences between you and your grandparents in regard to choice of career?

3. Has one of your friends had a disagreement with his or her parents about career choice? What finally happened?

Language Practice

Fill in the blanks below with appropriate words from this list:

upset	impressed	stunned
intact	useless	quizzical
proud	intense	scared

My father was very _____ of my grades in science and wanted me

to be an engineer. When I came home one day and told him I wanted to be an

astronaut, he was _____ . "Aren't you _____ ?" I asked.

"Aren't you _____ ?" he asked. "No," I said. "I can become an astro-

naut and then I can make a living in politics." The look on his face was

_____ . He said, "I certainly don't think it's _____ work, but

I'm afraid that you may not come back _____ ."

Fill in the blanks in the sentences below with phrases from this list. You
may use a word more than once.

> take over   do for a living
> make a living   take (someone or something) seriously
> take the credit for

1. If the political leaders in charge now do not solve our economic problems,

    the army may _____ the country.

2. I don't know why you think I'm joking when I say that I want to become

    an astronaut. Please, _____ me _____ .

3. I know what you _____ and I appreciate your offer, but I don't

    want to be a baker. I can _____ as an astronaut.

4. My mother wants to _____ my improvement; she says I got better

    because she gave me chicken soup.

5. Years ago, a son was often expected to _____ his father's business

    and _____ from it.

Combine phrases from Column A and Column B into sentences and write them below in paragraph form.

A	**B**
My father was	he was upset.
My father introduced me	every evening except Saturday.
His brothers were	a baker.
When I was fifteen I worked in my father's bakery	"but bakers always make a living."
He assumed	to his customers as "My son, the poet."
But when I told him I wanted to be a poet,	I would work in the bakery when I graduated.
"Poets starve," he said,	bakers, too.

_____

_____

_____

_____

_____

_____

_____

Complete each paragraph using your own words and ideas.

1. (someone) asked me for advice about _____

    _____

    I told them that _____

    _____

2. My father (or mother or brother or sister) assumed that I would _____

_____

but I _____

_____

3. _____

_____

_____

_____

I must have made the right decision.

4. _____

_____

_____

_____

My father (or mother) must have been stunned.

Write a paragraph that describes the occupations of several members of your family. Begin with a grandparent.

_____

_____

_____

_____

_____

_____

Follow-up Activities

1. Consult your classmates to find out (1) what careers they are interested in and (2) why they chose those careers.

2. There are many careers that did not exist twenty-five years ago. List five of these careers below and then compare your lists with those of other students.

    _____   _____   _____   _____   _____

3. "In" jokes are jokes or situations that are funny only to members of a particular group, such as a class or a family. If you know an "in" joke, describe it.

4. Light is a commercial artist. He describes some of his activities (designs covers, chooses type, places photographs, and so on). Choose a job with which you are familiar and list the tasks it requires.

Topics for Further Discussion or Writing

1. To what extent do children do the same work as their parents in your country?

2. What is the work pattern in your family? Will the children be doing the same work as the parents? Is what you want to do different from what your parents want you to do? What is your grandparents' attitude toward your career possibilities?

3. What are the advantages and disadvantages of working with a relative?

_____

Romantic Love: Asian and American

Before You Read

In this article George Theodorson reports on his survey of approximately 4,000 young people to find out their attitudes toward love and marriage.

Think About It

What do you think should be the basis of a marriage?

Do people of different backgrounds have different attitudes toward love and marriage? Can you think of some examples?

Romantic Love: Asian and American

George Theodorson

1   Traditionally, Americans and Asians have had very different ideas about love and marriage. Americans believe in "romantic" marriage — a boy and girl are attracted to each other, fall in love, and decide to marry each other. Asians, on the other hand, believe in *contractual* marriage — the parents of the bride and groom decide on the marriage, stating the terms of the agreement; the bride and groom may never meet until their wedding day; and love — if it ever develops — is supposed to follow marriage, not precede it. Generation after generation of Asian men and women have entered matrimony by way of the more business-like arrangements of the marriage contract.

2   Since the end of World War II, however, great changes have swept over Asia. Rapid urbanization, industrialization, and Westernization have sparked major social changes and broken down old traditions, taboos, and customs. Not the least of the many influences challenging the old culture of Asia are the Western-style mass media: the American-made movies, books, magazines, and "pop" tunes which are now seen and heard from Tokyo to Timbuktu. They all carry glamorous glimpses of American romantic love.

3   It is not surprising, therefore, that some important writers and politicians in these Asian countries have denounced the American influence as subversive and degrading. While the popular journalists may claim it is giving local youth unrealistic expectations of marriage, political and religious authorities see a much greater danger. They fear American-style romanticism will undermine the foundations of the family; and, of course, the *family* is the basic unit in any nation's social or political system.

4   This study, while neither defending nor attacking the romantic view of marriage, asks whether this American attitude is really replacing more traditional customs in East Asia. In other words, can rapid industrialization and urbanization actually affect the attitudes of youth toward love and marriage, and will young people discard centuries of traditions for customs only read about in books or seen in the movies?

5   To help answer these questions, a survey was made of approximately 4,000 American, Singapore Chinese, Burmese, and Indian young people to determine their attitudes toward love and marriage. If Westernization has really led the young people of East Asia to accept the romantic view of marriage, then their views of marriage should be the same as the views of their American counterparts.

MEASURING ROMANTICISM

6   The data for measuring the romanticism of Asian youth were drawn from responses to a questionnaire designed for college students. College students were chosen especially for this study because they are

the most Westernized group in their countries; thus they are the most likely to have been influenced by ideas of romantic love. The questionnaires were written in English; thereby further guaranteeing that the people who answered them were both well educated and familiar with Western ideas, customs, and literature.

7   The students answering the questionnaire included 748 men and 576 women from two universities in the northeastern United States, 249 men and 237 women from the largest university in Burma, 1,038 men and 202 women from nine universities in northern India, and 510 Chinese men and 287 Chinese women from the university and three other institutes in Singapore, making a total of 3,847 students.

8   The students received identical sets of statements concerning some aspect of marriage. They were asked to indicate after each of five key statements whether they 1) strongly agreed, 2) agreed, 3) were uncertain, 4) disagreed, or 5) strongly disagreed with it. The key statements themselves were carefully designed to measure for crucial values distinguishing romantic from contractual views of marriage.

9   The first of these key statements was this: "The person I marry must be physically attractive." This statement was designed to measure how strongly the person believed in the American idea that physical appearance, or "sex appeal," is one of the most important ingredients in any romance.

10   Another of the American romantic ideas is that a wife should continue to be attractive after marriage. To measure this the students were asked to agree or disagree with a second key statement: "A woman should be as concerned about her appearance after marriage as she was before."

11   The third key statement read: "Sometimes it is wise not to completely confide in your mate." If a student agreed with this statement, it meant that he believed in the contractual ideal of never sharing certain thoughts with one's spouse; if he disagreed with the statement, it indicated that he believed in the romantic ideal of "perfect companionship" where the husband and wife share every thought and action, withholding no secrets, no matter how small.

12   Fourth, the questionnaire measured the students' attitudes about the equality of sacrifice in marriage. The American, or romantic, view is that a husband and wife must be equal partners. In other words, neither man nor wife should be expected to sacrifice more than the other. The traditional Eastern view, however, was that the woman should give up everything for her husband. The students were therefore asked whether they agreed or disagreed with the key statement: "Generally speaking, a woman has to sacrifice more in marriage than a man."

13   The last key statement measured the students' belief in the romantic ideal of a marriage of trust based on love. They were asked if they agreed that: "A husband is obliged to tell his wife where he has been if he comes home late." Agreement meant a contractual view, disagreement a romantic view of marriage (Table 1).

TABLE 1 Acceptance of Romanticism

Men	Americans	Singapore Chinese	Burmese	Indians
1. Physical attraction as a criterion of partner choice	133	103	—	75
2. Physical attractiveness of wife after marriage	164	84	88	65
3. Marriage as companionship: mutual confiding	168	100	86	54
4. Marriage as partnership: equality of sacrifice	160	94	88	63
5. Trust in the husband	137	81	80	87
Women				
1. Physical attraction as a criterion of partner choice	130	78	—	44
2. Physical attractiveness of wife after marriage	134	81	77	57
3. Marriage as companionship: mutual confiding	138	67	65	81
4. Marriage as partnership: equality of sacrifice	158	62	76	17
5. Trust in the husband	161	54	43	57

Each number in the table is an *index*, not a total of the students' answers. (The index numbers are based on the totals, which are put through certain statistical steps.) The advantage of an index is that higher index numbers indicate more Westernized answers; lower figures mean less of Western influence. Thus the figures show that the Singapore Chinese are more Westernized in their attitudes to love and marriage than are the Burmese, for the numbers are lower in the Burmese columns, and that Indian women, whose index numbers are the lowest of all, are the least Westernized.

ROMANTIC RESPONSES . . . AND RESULTS

14 The American students were, of course, the most romantic (Table 1). While none of the Asian students were as romantic as the Americans, the Singapore Chinese were more romantically inclined than the Burmese, who, in turn, were significantly more romantic than the Indians. Following is a summary of each group's responses to the key statements:

15 *Physical Attractiveness:* Indian and Chinese students were definitely less concerned than American students with physical attractiveness when choosing a wife or husband. In Burma, the question was not asked.

16 The American students were much more concerned than the other students that a wife maintain her beauty and glamour after marriage; in fact, they almost unanimously agreed that "a woman should be as concerned with her appearance after marriage as she was before." Although none of the Asian students were opposed to this idea, none of them felt as strongly as did the American students. Again, it simply was less important to them.

17   *Confiding*: Similarly, few Asian students, in any group, agreed with the American students' view that wives and husbands should share all thoughts. In fact, a majority of Indians, Burmese, and Chinese actually thought it was better and wiser for a couple not to discuss certain matters or share certain thoughts. Indeed, this is a belief characteristic of the old contractual view of marriage. A particularly large proportion of Indian men (82 percent) agreed that it was unwise to confide in their wives. . . .

18   *Partnership of Equals*: Again, the majority of Asian students reject the American, or romantic, view that marriage is a "partnership of equals," demanding no more or no less from each of the partners. An overwhelming majority of the Indian students (including some 90 percent of the women) agreed that "a woman has to sacrifice more in a marriage than a man." Although the responses of the Chinese and Burmese students were not as strong, they still were considerably less inclined to the romantic sentiment than were the American students.

19   *Trust Built on Love*: Significantly, more Asian students than American students agreed that "a husband is obliged to tell his wife where he has been if he comes home late." Again, this indicates a major difference between the American's romantic views about marriage and the Asian's contractual views about marriage.

20   The American wife, for example, trusts her husband to "do the right thing" because "he loves her," not because "he has to." The Asian husband, on the other hand, views the *contract* of marriage almost as a business-like agreement, and he respects its clauses and agreements because society expects him to do so. The Asian wife, in turn, feels she can demand a record of her husband's activities, if she suspects the contract has been broken.

21   In actual practice, of course, American husbands do not always keep their promises and American wives are not always happy when their husbands come home late. But the American students apparently idealized the situation. This means they responded to the statement with an image of the "perfect marriage" in mind — an image created by a tradition of romanticism. The Asian students, by contrast, responded to the statement with a more practical image in mind — an image based on a tradition of contractualism.

22   *The Results*: By any measurement of romanticism's four values — 1) physical attractiveness before and after marriage, 2) confiding, 3) equal partnership, and 4) trust based on love — Asian young people are far from being as romantic as their American counterparts, even today.

Comprehension

1. What were the traditional attitudes of Americans and Asians toward love and marriage?

2. Why did the author think that a survey of these attitudes would be useful?

3. What questions does the author think the survey will answer?

4. Why did the author choose college students?

5. Describe the method used in the survey.

6. Describe some of the survey's findings.

Discussion

1. The survey was done in the 1960s. Do you think the results would be similar today?

2. What do you think the results would be if the survey were done in your country?

3. Is the basis of marriage a subject that is discussed in your family? How do young people in your country get their ideas about love and marriage?

4. What do you think of surveys as a way to find out what people believe? Are there other ways to get this information?

Language Practice

Find the meaning of the underlined words in the following sentences. Then rewrite each sentence substituting appropriate words or phrases for the underlined ones.

1. Love is supposed to follow marriage, not <u>precede</u> it. (See paragraph 1.)

_____

_____

2. <u>Rapid</u> changes after World War II have affected the old traditions and <u>customs</u>. (See paragraph 2.)

_____

_____

3. Western movies and magazines provide a glamorous <u>glimpse</u> of romantic love. (See paragraph 2.)

_____

4. Some important Asian writers have <u>denounced</u> the American influence as subversive and <u>degrading</u>. (See paragraph 3.)

_____

_____

5. They fear that American-style romanticism will <u>undermine</u> the <u>foundations</u> of the family. (See paragraph 3.)

_____

_____

6. Will young people <u>discard</u> centuries of tradition? (See paragraph 4.)

_____

7. A survey was made to <u>determine</u> their attitudes toward love and marriage. (See paragraph 5.)

_____

_____

8. The statements were designed to measure <u>crucial</u> values. (See paragraph 8.)

_____

9. A husband <u>is obliged</u> to tell his wife where he has been. (See paragraph 13.)

_____

10. They agreed it was unwise <u>to confide in their wives</u>. (See paragraph 11.)

_____

_____

With which of the situations in the right-hand column can you associate the sentences on the left below? Circle your answers and be prepared to defend them.

1. Changes swept over Asia.

    a. Military governments were overthrown in six countries.

    b. The building was dirty, but they found some brooms and cleaned it up.

    c. The general thought very carefully about his decision to change the form of government.

2. Traditions have broken down.

    a. They decided to get married in the same church where his parents were married.

    b. We don't know why we celebrate that holiday.

    c. As a result of the accident, he broke his leg.

3. A woman should give up everything for her husband.

    a. Jean told Michael not to send her so many presents.

    b. If you sell your drums, I'll stop smoking.

    c. When Lawrence died, his wife inherited everything.

For some people, physical attractiveness is a *criterion* for the choice of a partner. Demonstrate your understanding of the word *criterion* by answering the following questions.

1. What is your criterion for success in life? _____

_____

2. What is your criterion for a good movie? _____

_____

Theodorson presented the students in the survey with a set of *key* statements. Combine the word *key* with the words on the left below to make phrases. Then, on the lines provided, use each phrase in a sentence that shows its meaning.

EXAMPLE: person *In many universities, the secretary of a department knows everything. He or she is a key person.*

1. decision   _____

_____

2. position   _____

_____

3. word   _____

_____

The word *data* is used frequently in surveys and research. On the lines below, give some examples of data, using your classroom as a source of information.

_____

_____

Using your own words, summarize the ideas in the selection's first paragraph.

_____

_____

The author uses the phrase "to do the right thing." Briefly describe a situation in which a husband or wife does the right thing.

_____

_____

In a paragraph, describe two characteristics necessary for a good marriage. You may want to use some of these words:

partnership	equals	trust	sacrifice
companionship	attraction	confide in	

_____

_____

_____

_____

_____

Complete this paragraph in your own words.

Many old traditions in my country have been discarded. For example, ___

_____

_____

But some traditions are still alive. _____

_____

_____

Choose one of the survey's "key statements" with which you agree or disagree. On the lines below, tell why you agree or disagree.

_____

_____

Follow-up Activities

1. Consult Table 1 and write a summary of some differences in responses among (1) the national groups and (2) men and women in the same national group.

2. Survey your classmates or friends, asking, Do you want to get married? You might also ask, Do you think you will get married? Be prepared to report your results to the class.

3. Choose a key statement and do a survey, using the five responses that the author established. Compare your results with those of other students.

Herbert Hahn

Before You Read

Andy Rooney is a television commentator who usually talks about the pleasures and problems of everyday life. Here he tells us about a teacher that he liked very much.

Think About It

Are there things that you wish you had said to someone but didn't?

Why didn't you say those things?

Herbert Hahn

Andy Rooney

1 He lived only a thirty-five-cent phone call away, but I never called him. No one influenced my life more than he did. Now he's gone and I don't think I ever told him.

2 I worked late yesterday and didn't get home until after eight. We had a quick dinner and it was too late to start anything else, so at ten I got into bed with the newspaper I'd never taken the time to read. The economic news was bad and the Giants' coach said he wasn't discouraged. I leafed through to the obituary page and my eye caught the little headline in boldface type.

3 I dropped the paper to the floor next to the bed and stared at the ceiling. Mr. Hahn was dead. *Why* hadn't I called him? I was surprised to find myself crying. I hadn't really seen Mr. Hahn for forty years, didn't even know he was "Dr. Hahn" now, but I had thought of him on almost every one of the days of those forty years.

4   My memory of exactly what he was like in school was incredibly clear to me. I remember every mannerism, the way he pulled at the crease of the knee of his pants when he sat on the edge of his desk. I even remember that he only had two suits in 1936. One was his old suit and one was his good suit. He wore the old one for two days every other week when the good one was at the cleaners. He only made twenty-seven hundred dollars a year teaching history in Albany, N.Y., then and clothes were not a top priority of his.

5   He left Albany in about 1945 to teach at a good private school in New Jersey, and I wasn't surprised that the obituary called him an English teacher. It didn't really matter what Mr. Hahn's class was called. He taught life and his subject was of secondary importance. When we were fourteen and fifteen, he talked to us as though we were human beings, not children. He talked about everything in class, and just to make sure we knew he didn't think he was omnipotent, he often followed some pronouncement he'd made about government or politics by saying, "And don't forget you heard it from the same teacher who predicted in 1932 that Hitler would get nowhere in Germany."

6   How many teachers do you have in your life? I lay there wondering last night. Between grade school, high school and college, if you're lucky enough to go to college, I suppose you have about fifty teachers. Is that about right?

7   I don't remember much about some of mine, and nothing about what they were trying to teach me, but of those fifty, I had five who were very good and two who were great. Mr. Hahn was one of those.

8   He didn't do a lot of extra talking, but when he talked he was direct and often brilliant. He was the only genuine philosopher I ever knew. He wasn't a teacher of philosophy, but a living, breathing philosophizer. He exuded wisdom, concern for the world and quite often a bad temper. Idiots irritated him, and it annoyed him when teenagers acted younger than he was treating them.

9   I went to the service for him today. I don't know why, really. There was no one there I knew, and one phone call over the years would have meant more to him. A minister spoke, but it was standard stuff, and Mr. Hahn was not what most people would call a religious person, even though he wrote a book called *The Great Religions: Interpretations*.

10   A young woman who taught with him spoke, and she brought the tears back to my eyes. He had touched her life in the 1970s as he had touched mine in the 1930s.

11   Mr. Hahn could have taught at any college in the country, but he chose to stay at the secondary level. He didn't think teaching college-age people was any more important than teaching boys and girls fourteen to eighteen. He was the kind of person who gave teachers the right to be proud to be teachers.

12   I just wish I'd called or written to tell him how much he meant to my life.

Comprehension

1. What did the author regret about his relationship with Mr. Hahn?

2. Why did the author write about Mr. Hahn's clothes?

3. Why was the name of the subject that Mr. Hahn taught not important to the author?

4. What was Mr. Hahn's attitude toward himself?

5. What kinds of students bothered Mr. Hahn?

6. Approximately how many years did Mr. Hahn teach?

7. Why didn't Mr. Hahn teach at the college level?

Discussion

1. What do you remember best about the teachers you have had?

2. What do you think is the most important quality in a teacher?

3. Why is it that we so often don't say the things that we should?

Language Practice

Match each sentence on the left below with the item on the right that has a similar meaning. Circle your answer.

1. No one influenced my life more than he did.

   a. I had a great influence on his life.

   b. He had a great influence on my life.

   c. No one had a great influence on my life.

2. He wore the old suit for two days every other week when the good one was at the cleaners.

   a. He cleaned his good suit every week.

   b. He wore his old suit four times in two weeks.

   c. He wore his good suit every day except for two days every other week.

3. It really didn't matter what Mr. Hahn's class was called.

   a. Mr. Hahn did not like to name his class.

   b. No one knew what the matter was with Mr. Hahn's class.

   c. What Mr. Hahn's class was called was not important.

4. It annoyed him when teenagers acted younger than he was treating them.

   a. He treated the teenagers as though they were older.

   b. He treated the teenagers as idiots.

   c. He treated the teenagers as though they were younger.

5. There was no one there I knew.

   a. I knew that there wasn't anyone there.

   b. I didn't know anyone who was there.

   c. I knew no one who wasn't there.

The author writes, "He talked to us as though we were human beings, not children." *As though* compares a situation that exists with one that doesn't. "I ate as though I was hungry" means that I wasn't hungry but I pretended to be hungry. Use the phrase *as though* in two sentences.

1. _____

2. _____

The author describes Mr. Hahn's mannerisms. Check the meaning of the word *mannerism*. Then briefly describe the mannerisms of someone you know.

_____

_____

_____

_____

Combine phrases from Column A and Column B into sentences and write them below in paragraph form.

A	**B**
I worked late yesterday	and began to cry.
When I reached the obituary page	and then I got into bed and read the newspaper.
The political news was bad,	but I had always thought about him.
I dropped the paper to the floor	I saw a headline with my teacher's name in it.
I was surprised	but the President wasn't discouraged.
We had a quick dinner,	so I didn't get home until after eight.
I hadn't seen my teacher for many years,	to find myself crying.

_____

_____

_____

_____

_____

_____

_____

Mr. Hahn had a "concern for the world." What do you think that means? What subjects do you think Mr. Hahn would be discussing today? List some of them below.

_____   _____

_____   _____

Choose someone who has meant a lot to you and describe him or her in four or five sentences below. You might want to use some of these words:

influence	brilliant	priority
proud	importance	concern
genuine	wisdom	memory
lucky		

_____

_____

_____

_____

_____

Follow-up Activities

1. Below list your priorities for the next five years. Then compare your list with those of other students.

   _____

   _____

   _____

2. Choose five sentences from the text and write them below. In each, leave out a key word or words that sometimes cause problems for learners of English. For example, "The news _____ bad." Many students guess that *news* is plural. Then ask a classmate to fill in the blanks. Compare your "test" with those of other students.

   a. _____

   b. _____

   c. _____

   d. _____

   e. _____

3. Often we don't tell people what we want to tell them; the author never called Mr. Hahn to tell him how much he liked him. Think of a similar situation in your own life. Describe the situation, telling what you did say and what you think you should have said.

Chapter Review

1. Compare the selections by Toth and Rooney, who both write about the importance of human relationships. In what ways are their ideas related?

2. Both Light and Theodorson wrote about the relationships between parents and children. This is a common topic in the popular and classical literature of many countries and a common theme for contemporary television programs. Choose a program or a work of literature with this theme and be prepared to discuss it.

Work 7

Most of us have to work. But what kinds of jobs are available now?
How important should work be in our lives? What kinds of conditions
do we want when we work? The authors of the readings in this chapter
try to answer these questions.

Balancing Love and Work — It May Save Your Life

Before You Read

In this newspaper interview, Jay Rohrlich, a psychiatrist, tells about the
importance of work in our lives.

Think About It

Do you know any people who seem to be working all the time? Why do
they do it?

How important do you think work will be in your life?

Balancing Love and Work — It May Save Your Life

Linda Matchan

1 New York psychiatrist Jay B. Rohrlich points out the dark side of the
   role of work in our lives with this tragic story about a friend:

2   His friend was chief of surgery at a major metropolitan hospital. He had a large private practice, wrote and published extensively, and often traveled across the country to attend professional meetings. He loved his work, leaving the house at 5:45 each morning and rarely getting home again until nine in the evening. He spent the two-and-a-half-hour daily train commute into the city reading and writing. Sleep, he felt, was unproductive.

3   On weekends, when he wasn't attending conferences or writing, he tackled a variety of projects around the house — building a tree house with his kids, for example, or rotating the tires on his cars. He once confided to Rohrlich that, as Fridays approached, he grew tense and anxious if he had no structured activity lined up to occupy the next 48 hours.

4   He rarely took vacations, and when he did they were short and not really vacations at all, since he spent much of his time reading and writing professional material. Sometimes, according to Rohrlich, he would seem to "get sick" before or during the vacation. Other times some urgent problem inevitably came up to destroy his travel plans.

5   Finally, under protest from his wife, he agreed to a three-week vacation away from his work. They flew to the Caribbean. There he had a heart attack on the beach and died.

6   Rohrlich says his friend was an example of someone literally addicted to his work. He believes the man died, in part, from the stress of not working.

7   Work addiction is as real and tangible a phenomenon as addiction to alcohol or to drugs, Rohrlich maintains.

8   Although he says the psychiatric profession has paid little attention to the subject of work addiction, people who are hooked on work are "very common" and span all occupations and social classes. Not all work addicts are ambitious, says Rohrlich. Some don't want to work incessantly. They just aren't able to stop.

9   It's Rohrlich's contention that well-integrated lives call for a healthy balance between what he sees as the two basic requirements of human existence: work and love. "But love and work are very different. Work is goal-directed and oriented to the future, and love is the essence of the present."

10   He stresses that it's not necessarily bad when people decide they want their work to take precedence in their lives over family or social life. "What's bad is when we make the choice out of compulsion and not free will. It's not necessarily bad for people to make the decision to exclude love from their lives if it's a free and honest choice."

11   He's found that many work addicts he's associated with go through withdrawal symptoms when, for some reason, they try to stop working. They experience extreme anxiety, depression, psychosomatic illness, migraines, ulcers, hypertension, or even heart disease. He believes that in extreme cases, such as his friend's, forced relaxation can even be fatal.

12   For such people, work is not just a state of employment but a state of mind, Rohrlich says. These people are not simply devoted to work; they can't function without it.

13   He says work addicts work even during their leisure activities. They can't enjoy a sunset without photographing it, can't take a vacation without their attaché case, can't play a game without working to improve their speed or score. They may eat, sleep, even make love, precisely by the clock, since they're unable to savor or appreciate spontaneous pleasures. Everything has to have a point. Everything has to be goal directed.

Comprehension

Expand your understanding of the article's main ideas.

1.   What kind of work did Rohrlich's friend do?

2.   What was unusual about the attitude of Rohrlich's friend toward vacations?

3.   What was the cause of the friend's death, according to Rohrlich?

4.   What does Rohrlich believe to be the basis of a well-integrated life?

5.   How does Rohrlich differentiate between love and work? Do you agree?

6.   What are "withdrawal symptoms"?

7.   What do work addicts do during their leisure time?

8.   Does Rohrlich think that it is bad to exclude love from one's life? Explain by referring to the reading.

Applications

Relate the article to events in your own life.

1.   Do you think the attitude toward work described in the article occurs worldwide?

2.   What are your family members' attitudes toward work?

3.   To what extent do you balance your work (or study) and your leisure? How?

4.   Besides work, what are some other things to which people can become addicted?

Their Work Is Play

Before You Read

In this selection, Tim Smight interviews three college graduates about their jobs and how they found them. The selection includes quotations from the graduates.

Think About It

What kinds of jobs do people in your field of work or study want?

How do people usually get jobs in your country?

Their Work Is Play

Tim Smight

PAUL WOESSNER, BALLOONIST

1 "I think I like the pure joy of ballooning the most," says Iowa State University graduate Paul Woessner. "You're flying around in this huge toy, and everyone who spots you becomes an instant kid."

2 At age 25, Paul is the current world champion of ballooning. He's also vice president and co-founder of the world's largest ballooning concern, World Balloon Corporation of Albuquerque, New Mexico.

3 "We fly promotions, give rides and lessons, sell and repair balloons," says Paul. "Everything that can be done with balloons, we do."

4 He discovered ballooning six years ago when two "aeronauts" landed in his family's suburban Chicago yard. "They gave me a ride, and it was just a pure rush of excitement," Paul recalls. "The next day I sold my motorcycle and skis and started learning to fly." He soon bought his own balloon and began flying promotions at Iowa State, where he was a senior studying to become a veterinarian. It wasn't long before most of Paul's spare time was spent in the air.

5 "My interests just shifted to ballooning, and by the time I graduated, my G.P.A. was a hair too low for vet school," he recalls. While interviewing for work in the field of animal science, he was offered a job with an Illinois ballooning club as flight instructor.

6 That same summer Paul achieved national recognition by becoming the first balloonist to cross Lake Michigan. Within six months he'd moved to Albuquerque — where he won the biennial World Championships last year — and had started World Balloon Corporation.

7 When not involved in World Balloon activities, Paul spends a lot

of time competing and flying promotionally at fairs and races across the country. But he enjoys fun flying most of all.

8   "The freedom and the unpredictability of ballooning just can't be matched by anything else," Paul says. "You never know where you'll land, or who you'll meet, so each flight is unique and fresh. That's why I'll never tire of it." He currently plans to help start a professional racing circuit — and he sees a bright future for what he calls "the sport of the gods."

9   "I think ballooning is about to explode, especially after the Atlantic crossing. There's nothing I'd rather be doing in the way of employment. Sometimes it's very hard to believe this is my job — because it's so much fun."

CATHY GUISEWITE, CARTOONIST

10   Like many college students, Cathy Guisewite dreamed of a job that would offer independence, recognition and a chance to be creative. Three years after graduating with an English degree from the University of Michigan, she reached that goal — as the youngest nationally syndicated cartoonist in the country. Her daily strip, *Cathy*, runs in over 120 newspapers and is read by millions of people each day.

11   "I still freak out sometimes when I wake up in the morning and realize I'm a cartoonist," says Cathy, who entered the field in true Cinderella fashion two years ago. How did it happen?

12   "My mother had a lot to do with it," explains Cathy. "I was working for an advertising agency in Detroit as a writer, going through all the traumas of young adulthood. I used to send my mother stick-figure drawings of me in certain situations."

13   Cathy's mom thought the cartoons were good, and at her urging Cathy sent them to Universal Press, the syndicate that handles *Doonesbury* and *Ziggy*.

14   "Two days later they sent me a contract. Suddenly I was a cartoonist — and I could hardly draw!"

15   For a year Cathy kept her ad agency job — she'd risen to vice president — and tried to work on her new strip nights and weekends. "The pace got to be too much, so last year I quit the agency to work full time on the strip," she says.

16   Indeed, the cartoon's title is not coincidental. Much of what befalls Cathy-the-cartoon is taken from the real-life experiences of Cathy-the-cartoonist.

17   "The strip is about being young and female in the '70s, with the conflict between traditional roles and the new feminism," says Cathy, now 27. "A lot of what happens to the 'Cathy' happened to me first."

18   The young cartoonist works out of her Southfield, Michigan, condominium, and spends about two hours drawing each strip. She tries to keep three weeks ahead on the daily strip. "There's a good deal of pressure, since the strip is solely my responsibility," Cathy says. "But

I love doing it. Sometimes I miss working with other people, but this is quite a rewarding channel for self-expression. I want to keep it going as long as I can."

BOB OSBORNE, KILLER-WHALE TRAINER

19   Bob Osborne's teaching job requires patience, sensitivity — and raw nerve. For the past five years, Bob has trained the killer whales at San Diego's Sea World.

20   "I'm known as a 'behaviorist,' but basically I'm in charge of everything involving the whales," says Bob, 30. "I train them, feed them, play with them and perform with them.

21   "Fear? Let's just say I have a deep respect for the potential of the animals."

22   Although he holds an advanced degree in zoology from San Diego State, Bob got into this line of work in a roundabout way. "After I finished school, I worked for two years in business management," he explains. "I was miserable, trapped behind a desk. I applied for the job at Sea World because I wanted something unique, personal and outdoors."

23   Bob and his staff spend up to 12 hours a day working and performing with the park's four killer whales. They teach the whales tricks and routines that range from fetching objects to performing elaborate dance numbers.

24   "The whales are incredibly smart and curious," Bob says. "They don't have to channel their energies toward survival here, and that opens the door to more creative behavior. I try to establish a rapport with each animal. The idea is to teach them to perform *with* me, not *for* me."

25   Developing that cooperative method of instruction helped Bob overcome his initial apprehensions about the job.

26   "I was very intimidated at first. Killer whales have big mouths and big teeth. They have a bad reputation, and I felt very vulnerable in the water with them. But I soon learned they're not malicious at all."

27   Bob says he has no desire to quit or return to an office position. "I consider my job a rare privilege. I'm outside all day, and working with the whales really fascinates me. Few people in the world get an opportunity to work with such magnificent animals."

Comprehension

1. How does Paul's company get its income?

2. What does Cathy see as one disadvantage of her work?

3. What is Bob's attitude toward killer whales?

4. For the people described in this selection, what was the relationship between their education and their jobs?

5. How did these people find their jobs?

6. What do these people like about their jobs?

Discussion

1. Most available jobs are not "play." How do people with ordinary jobs make them more pleasant?

2. What would your ideal job be?

3. What kinds of jobs do you expect to find available when you start your search?

Language Practice

Read the following definitions. Then fill in the blanks with an appropriate word from the reading.

1. a legal agreement in which people agree to do something (See paragraph 14.) _____

2. a person in the last year of high school or university (See paragraph 4.) _____

3. a fixed and regular way of doing things (See paragraph 23.) _____

4. a doctor who works with animals (See paragraph 4.) _____

5. an apartment building that is owned by its residents (See paragraph 18.) _____

6. an object (a doll, a ball, and so on) that children play with (See paragraph 1.) _____

7. a competition that involves speed (See paragraph 7.) _____

8. a place, often at the back of a house, where children can play or people can plant a garden (See paragraph 4.) _____

9. a way of doing things that is not direct (See paragraph 22.) _____

10. an area where people live outside the central city (See paragraph 4.) _____

For each of the following verbs, first write its definition and then write sentences using it that answer the questions on the left, as in the example.

EXAMPLE: train

Definition: *to teach, to instruct, to give practice*

Who? What?   *Experienced doctors train new doctors.*
                Circus workers train animals to do tricks.

Where?   *Teachers train students in schools.*
                Managers train people in offices.

When?   *People are trained at the beginning of*
                a new job or before they start working.

Why?   *People are trained so they can do*
                their job well.

Now define and illustrate the meaning of the two verbs below.

VERB: compete

Definition: _____

Who? What?   _____

               _____

Where?   _____

               _____

When?   _____

               _____

Why?   _____

               _____

VERB: shift

Definition: _____

Who? What?   _____

               _____

Where?   _____

  _____

When?   _____

  _____

Why?   _____

  _____

Choose the appropriate forms of the words in each of the following sets and write them in the blanks below.

1. to tire   tiring   tired

In addition to spending 40 hours at their workplaces, some people bring work home. Take teachers, for example. Their work is _____ . They work at school and at home. "Although my work _____ me, I wouldn't want to do anything else. I often feel _____ when I get home, but I also feel good helping others to learn," says Mr. Appleton, a high school physics teacher.

2. to fascinate   fascination   fascinating   fascinated

"Meeting famous people _____ me," a secretary who works in Washington, D.C., said. "Although I don't get paid very much, and I hate to type, my job holds a certain _____ I couldn't get elsewhere. I meet many _____ people: senators, foreign dignitaries, and even movie stars." This young lady is so _____ with her job that she recently turned down a better-paying job in New York City.

3. to excite   excitement   exciting   excited

"The _____ of racing down a mountain at 60 or 70 mph is out of this world," says Bob, a ski instructor in Vermont. Bob is lucky because skiing has begun to _____ more and more people of all ages everywhere there is snow, natural or man-made. Everyone finds it _____ to ski down a mountain or even a small hill. Bob is especially _____ , because if skiing becomes a common form of recreation, he'll have a good job.

Below is a list of important events in Paul Woessner's life and career in ballooning. The list is not in chronological order. Arrange the list in order of time by writing numbers next to the events. Number 1 is filled in for you. Be prepared to give reasons for your arrangement by referring to the reading.

_____ Started the World Balloon Corporation

_____ Sold his motorcycle and skis

_____ Began flying promotions at Iowa State University

_____ Got a job with an Illinois ballooning club

_____ Plans to help start a professional racing circuit

_____ Started learning to fly

_____ Became the first balloonist to cross Lake Michigan

___1___ Got a ride from two balloonists who landed in his family's backyard

_____ Graduated from Iowa State University

_____ Moved to Albuquerque, New Mexico

_____ Bought his own balloon

On the following lines write a chronologically ordered paragraph using the information above. In your paragraph, combine answers 2 and 3, 4 and 5, 6 and 7 by using the connectors in the following list.

after   soon
after six months   then
at the moment   the next day
during that summer

_____

_____

_____

_____

_____

_____

_____

_____

Find evidence in the reading to support the following statements and write the evidence on the lines below.

EXAMPLE: According to Paul, the future of ballooning looks good. (See paragraph 9.)

I think ballooning is about to explode, especially after the Atlantic crossing.

1. Killer whales can do both simple and complex tasks. (See paragraph 23.)

_____

_____

2. Cathy was quite successful in her former job with the ad agency. (See paragraph 15.)

_____

_____

3. Paul enjoys speed. (See paragraphs 7 and 8.)

   _____

   _____

4. Bob never enjoyed being an office worker. (See paragraph 22.)

   _____

   _____

5. Cathy liked her ad agency job because she enjoys the company of other
   people. (See paragraph 18.)

   _____

   _____

For each of the following expressions, write a sentence describing an event
in your own life.

can't be matched   in charge of   opens the door   in a roundabout way

1. _____

2. _____

3. _____

4. _____

Follow-up Activities

1. Choose a career field in which you are interested (for example, medicine or
   marketing). Prepare a list of jobs related to that field. Compare your list
   with those of other students.

2. Prepare a résumé (a summary of your background and experience) for yourself. Include information about personal data (age, address, and so on) education, work experience, and special interests.

3. Look at job advertisements in a newspaper. Collect information on: categories of jobs available, training required for jobs, salaries and working conditions, and job features that advertisers emphasize.

4. Do you have strong labor unions in your country? Consult your classmates about unions in their country and prepare a report about advantages and disadvantages of unions.

5. Locate an article or book on careers or job counselors. Be ready to report on an aspect of the subject that interested you.

Topics for Further Discussion or Writing

1. Compare job opportunities in two countries.

2. Consider the following questions as you discuss or write about work:

   a. How important is money to you?

   b. How important is power to you?

   c. How hard do you want to work?

   d. Do you prefer activities that have great rewards but a significant risk, or activities with smaller rewards but less risk?

   e. How important is job prestige to you?

   f. How important are location and environment?

   g. Do you like a structured or an unstructured work environment?

3. We get many of our ideas and impressions about contemporary life from television. How is work portrayed on the popular television comedies? How often are people shown at work? What do they do at work?

A New Set of Work Values

Before You Read

This article is from *Psychology Today,* a popular magazine that responds to contemporary interest in psychology. Here, pollster Daniel Yankelovich writes on a topic relevant to all cultures — the changing values that accompany changing societies.

Think About It

What satisfactions do people in your country get from work?

Have you noticed any changing attitudes toward work in your country?

A New Set of Work Values

Daniel Yankelovich

1 A New Breed of Americans, born out of the social movements of the 60s and grown into a majority in the 70s, holds a set of values and beliefs so markedly different from the traditional outlook that they promise to transform the character of work in America in the 80s.

2 For most of this century (roughly up to 1970), the value system of most Americans centered around a number of powerful, culturally derived symbols which provided Americans with at least some of the essentials of psychological well-being. In particular, these symbols proved capable of giving people a sense of self-esteem, a clear identity, well-defined goals and values, a sense of effectiveness, and a conviction that one's private goals and behavior also contributed to the well-being of others.

3 Most of these symbols are strikingly middle-class in character. They became dominant values in the 1950s and 1960s as more people were able to move into the middle class through education, a booming economy, and a steady rise in the median income.

4 Some of the consequences of the old value system for the world of work can be summed up as follows:
- If women could afford to stay home and not work at a paid job, they did so.
- As long as a job provided a man with a decent living and some degree of economic security, he would put up with all its drawbacks, because it meant that he could fulfill his economic obligations to his family and confirm his own self-esteem as breadwinner and good provider.
- The incentive system — mainly money and status rewards — was successful in motivating most people.
- People were tied to their jobs not only by bonds of commitment to their family, but also by loyalty to their organizations.
- Most people defined their identity through their work role, subordinating and suppressing most conflicting personal desires.

5 Under the new value system, all these consequences of the old value system have already changed or are in the process of changing.

Three of the more striking manifestations of New Breed work-related values are (1) the increasing importance of leisure, (2) the symbolic significance of the paid job, and (3) the insistence that jobs become less depersonalized.

THE PURSUIT OF LEISURE

6 Along with family life, work and leisure always compete for people's time and allegiance. One or the other is usually the center of gravity; rarely does the individual strike an equal balance among all three. For the New Breed, family and work have grown less important and leisure more important.

7 This is not a purely American phenomenon. A recent study in Sweden produced a striking set of findings. When Swedish men, 18 to 55 years of age, were asked way back in 1955, "What gives your life the most meaning — your family, your work, or your leisure?," only 13 percent answered "leisure," 33 percent "work," and 45 percent their "family." In 1977, when the same question was asked of a new cross-section of Swedish men, the proportion of men naming work as the main source of meaning in life had been cut in half — from 33 percent to 17 percent. The position of family life had also *fallen* slightly — 45 percent to 41 percent. But dedication to leisure had more than doubled — from 13 percent to 27 percent!

THE PAID JOB AS A SYMBOL

8 If leisure grows more important for men in the pursuit of self-fulfillment, for New Breed women the symbolic significance of a paid job has greatly intensified. The money earned by the woman in most families has proven indispensable to maintaining a standard of living the family considers satisfactory.

9 For New Breed women, a paid job has become an almost indispensable symbol of self-worth. It is also a means of achieving autonomy and independence.

10 The woman with a paid job, however menial or poorly paid, feels that she no longer has to be totally dependent on the will and whim of a man. Divorce rates have shot up because divorce is now a practical option for millions of women. However, many women do not choose divorce because they are able to find work; they find work because they are forced to support themselves after their men leave.

THE PERSON COMES FIRST

11 More complex and intangible is the New Breed's refusal to subordinate their personalities to the work role.

12 One of the most striking characteristics of the old value system was the tendency for people to identify themselves with their work role. European visitors to the United States are often startled when Americans introduce themselves by saying, "I am a car dealer"; "I'm assistant manager of the local bank"; "I'm a housewife."

13   Today, the New Breed person demands that his or her individuality be recognized. In their eyes, when an individual is subordinated to his role, he somehow is turned into an object. In the new value system, the individual says, "I am more than my role. I am myself."

14   When asked which aspects of their work are becoming more important to them, people stress, "being recognized as an individual person." They also stress "the opportunity to be with pleasant people with whom I like to work."

15   In the 1980s, knowledge of how the changed American value system affects incentives and motivations to work hard may well become a key requirement for entering the ranks of top management. If this occurs, we shall see a New Breed of managers to correspond to the New Breed of employees.

16   The great changes taking place in the value system have consequences for *all* aspects of American life, but for none more than the workplace.

Comprehension

1. According to the author, what are some of the essentials of psychological well-being?

2. The author writes about "culturally derived symbols." To what is he referring?

3. What were the "old" values regarding work?

4. Why did the old values become dominant in the 1950s and 1960s?

5. What are some of the New Breed values?

6. The new values have become especially significant for women. Why?

Discussion

1. To what extent does this change of values apply to work in your country?

2. Is there evidence that people in your country are becoming more dedicated to leisure? What are they doing?

3. To what degree are significant jobs available for women in your country?

Language Practice

Substitute a word or phrase from the following list for an underlined word or phrase in the sentences below and rewrite the sentences.

menial	outlook	transform
indispensable	leisure	dedicate
	key	be capable of
	cross-section	
	incentive	

1. Some jobs that offer the worker good opportunities for <u>free time</u> also provide very little pay.

   _____

   _____

2. As an <u>encouragement</u> to better production, companies are offering their workers a share in ownership.

   _____

   _____

3. If we surveyed a <u>typical sample</u> of people living in the suburbs, we would probably find many families in which both the husband and wife work.

   _____

4. Although she had never worked in her own country, her <u>way of looking at things</u> changed quickly and she soon became a waitress.

   _____

   _____

5. The <u>element that is essential</u> to success in an organization may be the nature of the relationships among its workers.

   _____

   _____

6. We always argue when it's time to do the <u>low, domestic</u> jobs in the house.

_____

_____

7. Although I may <u>have the ability for</u> farm work, I could never get up at 4 A.M.

_____

_____

8. Changes in values may <u>change greatly</u> not only the workplace but all aspects of American life.

_____

_____

9. What is the one thing that you would find <u>absolutely essential</u> in a job?

_____

_____

10. While most of us give a large percentage of time to work, a growing number of people <u>devote</u> almost equal amounts of time to work and leisure.

_____

_____

_____

In the selection we find: "She no longer has to be totally dependent on the will and *whim* of a man." Check the meaning of *whim* and describe a whim of someone you know on the lines below.

_____

_____

_____

The author writes about the *drawbacks* of a job. Choose a job with which you are familiar and describe one or two of its drawbacks.

_____

_____

_____

Complete the following paragraph by adding an appropriate sentence.

People used to work to make money, to have an identity, or just to take up time. The financial motivation was probably the most common reason to work; the breadwinners had to provide food, clothing, and shelter for their families.

_____

_____

_____

The third reason was that there wasn't anything else to do. They didn't have the variety of leisure activities available today, so they worked to fill up the day.

Complete the paragraph that begins with the following sentence.

One of the most interesting differences between the value systems of the [put in the name of a people] and the [put in the name of another group] is their attitude toward work. _____

_____

_____

_____

_____

Combine the sentences in Columns A and B below into longer sentences. Use some of the following connectives. You may change the word order.

Connectives:

because	so
if	so . . . that
not only . . . but also	when

<table>
<tr><td align="center">**A**</td><td align="center">**B**</td></tr>
<tr><td>their values are different</td><td>the job loses its value</td></tr>
<tr><td>women did not have to work</td><td>it has become a way of achieving independence</td></tr>
<tr><td>a job has become a symbol of self-worth</td><td>he/she might not care about the job's drawbacks</td></tr>
<tr><td>divorce rates have increased</td><td>they will have difficulty if they get married</td></tr>
<tr><td>a boss doesn't recognize a worker's individuality</td><td>a woman is no longer dependent economically on a man</td></tr>
<tr><td>a person received enough income from a job</td><td>they stayed home</td></tr>
</table>

1. _____

_____

2. _____

_____

3. _____

_____

4. _____

_____

5. _____

_____

6. _____

_____

The following words may remind you of other words. List as many of these other words as you can. The first one is an example.

1. security *safe, job, secure, police, money, future.*

2. loyalty _____

3. middle-class _____

4. leisure _____

5. divorce _____

Fill in the blanks in the paragraph below with words from this list:

value	obligation	social	change
reward	self-esteem	economic	fulfill
income	individuality	intangible	recognize
status	motivation	traditional	
		successful	

A _____ is something that is important to us but as _____

conditions change, values _____ as well. For many people, the

_____ of work in the past was _____ ; when they brought

money home to their families they felt that they were _____ an eco-

nomic _____ . Another source of _____ was _____ ; if

someone was a professional, for example, that person would be considered

_____ . Nowadays the rewards of work are more _____ . Thus

if a manager does not _____ the _____ of a worker, the worker

may not have the _____ to work hard.

Follow-up Activities

1. Look at job advertisements in the newspaper. Notice to what extent the advertisers mention the new values — leisure, symbolic significance, individuality, and so on.

2. Survey about ten people. Ask them to list the job features below as Very Important, Not Very Important, or Not Important at All.

    a. Amount of information you get from your superiors about your job performance

    b. Amount of pay you get

    c. Amount of praise you get for a job well done

    d. Chances for getting a promotion

    e. Chances to accomplish something worthwhile

    f. Chances to do something that makes you feel good about yourself

    g. Chances to learn new things

    h. Chances to do things that you do best

    i. Opportunity to develop your skills and abilities

    j. Physical surroundings of your job

    k. The amount of freedom you have in your job

    l. The amount of fringe benefits you get

    m. The amount of job security you have

    n. The friendliness of people you work with

    o. The resources you have to do your job

    p. The respect you receive from people you work with

    q. The way you are treated by the people you work with

    r. Your chances for taking part in making decisions

Very Important	Not Very Important	Not Important at All
_____	_____	_____
_____	_____	_____

3. Complete the survey in no. 2 for yourself and rank the items, putting a 1 next to the feature you think most important, a 2 next to the second most important feature, and so on. Compare your results with those of your classmates.

4. Write a "future autobiography" — the story of your life looking back from a point 40 years in the future. Focus on your jobs and leisure. Write three paragraphs.

Getting Ready for the Jobs of the Future

Before You Read

In this article from *The Futurist,* Marvin Cetron notes that although technology is eliminating old jobs, it is also creating new jobs. He emphasizes the need to retrain workers.

Think About It

Which of today's jobs will be less needed in the future?

Name some jobs that didn't exist 20 years ago.

Getting Ready for the Jobs of the Future

Marvin J. Cetron

1 One thing is certain about tomorrow's job markets: dramatic shifts will occur in employment patterns. These changes are going to affect how we work and how we are educated and trained for jobs.

2 Major shifts in the job market won't necessarily mean major changes in the numbers of people employed. What the changes do mean is that many of the old jobs will disappear — and not just because of robots and computers. Manufacturing will provide only 11% of the jobs in the year 2000, down from 28% in 1980. Jobs related to agriculture will drop from 4% to 3%. The turn of the century will find the remaining 86% of the work force in the service sector, up from 68% in 1980. Of the service-sector jobs, half will relate to information collection, management, and dissemination.

3 Unemployment will be an ongoing problem. If the current recession were to end tomorrow, probably 1.2 million of the more than 11

million unemployed in the United States today would never be able to return to their old jobs in the automobile, steel, textile, rubber, or railroad industries. This loss of jobs is called structural unemployment.

4   Foreign competition in low-wage countries will eliminate about one-sixth of the 1.2 million jobs; another one-sixth will disappear because of the nationalization of many major industries in other countries that results in "dumping" of products on the U.S. market and undercutting American prices. "Computamation" (robotics, numerically controlled equipment, CAD/CAM [computer-aided design and computer-aided manufacturing], and flexible manufacturing) will assist in the demise of the remaining two-thirds of the jobs eliminated.

5   As this technological transition takes place, productivity will increase. For example, the use of a robot or a CAD/CAM system in the automotive industry can replace up to six workers if operated around the clock. Quality control increases fourfold, and scrap is reduced from 15% to less than 1%.

6   Japan already uses some of these new jobs and technology. It had no choice. Currently, it imports 96% of its energy. By the year 2000, that will rise to 98%. Eighty-seven percent of all of Japan's resources come from the outside. These statistics contributed to the decision to go robotic. But the essence of Japan's problem is that, between 1985 and 1990, 20% of the entire work force will retire at 80% of their base pay for the rest of their lives. Japan was forced to go robotic to remain competitive. The United States, too, will be filling many of today's blue-collar jobs with robots. The displaced workers will have to learn the new skills necessary to build and maintain the robots.

7   White-collar workers in the office of the future will also see some dramatic changes in their jobs. Currently, about 6,000 word lexicons — machines that type directly from speech — are in use. After a person dictates into the machine, a word lexicon types up to 97% of what was said. In addition, it can translate the material into nine languages, including Hebrew, which it types backward, and Japanese kanji symbols, which it types sideways and the user reads down the columns. Machines such as this will eliminate 50% of all clerical and stenographic jobs. But instead of going to an unemployment line, many of these workers may find jobs controlling the robots in factories using word-processing equipment.

8   As the types of jobs change, so will the definition of full employment. Currently, a 4.5% unemployment rate is considered full employment. But by 1990, 8.5% unemployment will be considered full employment. This figure is not as disturbing as it first appears, for at any given time 3.5% of the work force will be in training and education programs preparing for new jobs.

9   Workers will be able to take time out for retraining, in part, because of the shift in job patterns. In 1980, 45% of American households had two people working. In 1990, this proportion will increase to 65%, and in 2000, 75% of family units will have two incomes. This shift will allow easier transitions from the work force to training pro-

The Shifting Job Market

Some jobs that will be disappearing by 1990:

Occupation	% Decline in Employment
Linotype operator	−40.0
Elevator operator	30.0
Shoemaking machine operators	19.2
Farm laborers	19.0
Railroad car repairers	17.9
Farm managers	17.1
Graduate assistants	16.7
Housekeepers, private household	14.9
Childcare workers, private household	14.8
Maids and servants, private household	14.7
Farm supervisors	14.3
Farm owners and tenants	13.7
Timber cutting and logging workers	13.6
Secondary school teachers	13.1

Some jobs that will be growing until 1990:

Occupation	% Growth in Employment
Data processing machine mechanics	+157.1
Paralegal personnel	143.0
Computer systems analysts	112.4
Midwives	110.0
Computer operators	91.7
Office machine service technicians	86.7
Tax preparers	77.9
Computer programmers	77.2
Aero-astronautic engineers	74.8
Employment interviewers	72.0
Fast food restaurant workers	69.4
Childcare attendants	66.5
Veterinarians	66.1
Chefs	55.0

grams and back to the work force. Forecasts estimate that every four or five years one of the spouses or partners will leave the ranks of the employed to receive the additional knowledge and skills demanded by changes in technology and the workplace.

10   With these changes already taking place, workers must learn to do new jobs now and in the future. Vocational educators and trainers must gear up to provide this vital education and training to the work force of the next two decades — jobs related to robots, lasers, com-

puters, energy and battery technology, geriatric social work, hazardous-waste management, and biomedical electronics. (See table for some of the jobs that are disappearing and others that are growing in the shifting job market.)

NEW OCCUPATIONS FOR THE 1990s

11   The following occupations are among those that we can expect to become increasingly important:

12   *Energy Technician* (650,000 jobs) jobs will increase dramatically as new energy sources become marketable.

13   *Housing Rehabilitation Technician* (500,000 jobs). Intensifying housing demand will be met by mass production of prefabricated modular housing, using radically new construction techniques and materials.

14   *Hazardous Waste Management Technician* (300,000 jobs). Many years and billions of dollars may be required to clean up air, land, and water. New industries will add to the demand with new wastes.

15   *Industrial Laser Process Technician* (600,000 jobs). Laser manufacturing equipment and processes, including robotic factories, will replace much of today's machine and foundry tools and equipment.

16   *Industrial Robot Production Technician* (800,000 jobs). Extensive use of robots to perform computer-directed "physical" and "mental" functions will displace hundreds of thousands of workers. But new workers will be needed to ensure fail-proof operations of row after row of production robots.

17   *Materials Utilization Technicians* (400,000 jobs) must be trained to work with new materials being engineered and created to replace metals, synthetics, and other production substances unsuited for advanced manufacturing technologies.

18   *Genetic Engineering Technician* (250,000 jobs). Genetically engineered materials will be used extensively in three general fields: industrial products, pharmaceuticals, and agricultural products. New and modified substances will be produced under laboratory-like conditions in industrial mass-production quantities.

19   *Holographic Inspection Specialist* (200,000 jobs). Completely automated factories that use optical fibers for sensing light, temperature, pressure, and dimensions will transmit this information to optical computers to compare the data with stored holographic, three-dimensional images.

20   *Bionic-Medical Technician* (200,000 jobs). Mechanics will be needed to manufacture bionic appendages while other specialists work on highly sophisticated extensions of sensory and mental functions (seeing, hearing, feeling, speaking).

21   *Automotive Fuel Cell (Battery) Technicians* (250,000 jobs) will perform tests and services for new fuel cells and batteries used in vehicle and stationary operation, including residences.

22   *On-Line Emergency Technician* (400,000 jobs). Needs for paramedics will increase directly with the growth of the population and its aging. In forthcoming megalopolises and high-density residences, emergency medical treatment will be administered on the spot, aided by televised diagnoses and instruction from remote emergency medical centers.

23   *Geriatric Social Workers* (700,000 jobs) will be essential for the mental and social care of the nation's aging population.

24   *Energy Auditors* (180,000 jobs) will use the latest infrared devices and computer-based energy monitoring to work with architects, product engineers, and marketing staffs in the production, sales, and operation of energy conservation and control systems for housing, industrial plants, and machinery.

25   *Nuclear Medicine Technologists* (75,000 jobs) will work with medicines and serums using radioisotopes. As the isotopes are absorbed in tissues and muscles, diagnosticians can observe functions of normal and/or damaged tissues and organs and can determine treatment needs and responses to medication, thus reducing the need for surgery.

26   *Dialysis Technologists* (30,000 jobs) will operate new portable dialysis machines and the expected greater number of hospital dialysis machines.

27   *Computer-Assisted Design (CAD) Technician* (300,000 jobs). The computer can do more, better, and faster than traditional design methods. Whether designing modes of transportation, dwellings, or other products, CAD will affect education, employment, and ways of work more than any other single technology.

28   Most of these new jobs will require some kind of postsecondary vocational or technical training — training that is for the most part not now available.

Comprehension

1. What kinds of changes may take place in the job markets of the future?

2. What are some reasons that today's unemployed will not be able to return to their old jobs?

3. What's a CAD/CAM system?

4. According to the author, why was Japan forced to use robots so extensively?

5. What will be one of the most dramatic changes in the office of the future?

6. What does a "word lexicon" do? What does the machine have to be able to do?

7. Why is the author not disturbed by the idea of 8.5 percent unemployment in 1990?

8. Having two family incomes may bring a number of advantages; which advantage does the author point out?

Discussion

1. The chart in the reading shows a decline in employment in certain jobs. Why do you think these jobs will decline? (Consider them one at a time.)

2. What general suggestions would you give someone looking for a job? For example, how many job applications should be made? Is an interview important? How should people act in an interview?

Language Practice

Find the meaning of the underlined words in the following sentences. Then rewrite each sentence, substituting appropriate words or phrases from the reading for the underlined ones.

1. Unemployment will be a continuing problem. (See paragraph 3.)

   _____

   _____

2. In large institutions with many employees, the distribution of information is essential. (See paragraph 2.)

   _____

   _____

3. Because of changes in the job market, people who are being trained for a job now may have to be retrained later. (See paragraph 1.)

   _____

   _____

4. While the use of robots will <u>take away</u> some factory jobs, other jobs will become available for people to build and maintain the robots. (See paragraph 4.)

_____

_____

5. A <u>slowing down of business and industry</u> leads to unemployment. (See paragraph 3.)

_____

6. Since there are so many new occupations now, it might be a good idea to become a <u>counselor who advises about jobs</u>. (See paragraph 10.)

_____

_____

8. Each year there is an increasing need to store the <u>dangerous</u> waste products of our industries. (See paragraph 14.)

_____

_____

Check the meaning of the phrase "blue-collar job." On the lines below, list five jobs that you think would be blue-collar.

_____   _____

_____   _____

_____

Check the meaning of "white-collar job." On the lines below, list five jobs that you think would be white-collar.

_____   _____

_____   _____

_____

Choose an occupation that is expected to grow in the future. Write two or three sentences explaining the reasons for its growth.

_____

_____

_____

_____

There are many jobs not listed in the reading. Choose one of these jobs that you see as necessary in the future and tell why on the lines below. These words and phrases may give you ideas: food, clothing, shelter, sick people, old people, busy people, refrigerators, plumbing, cars, stoves.

_____

_____

_____

_____

We often use the indirect question structure as an object within a sentence:

These changes are going to affect how we work.
These changes are going to affect how we are educated.
We don't know when robots will be available for homework.
We don't know when robots will be available for housework.
She wondered why the job paid so little.

Complete the following sentences using a *how, when* or *why* structure.

1. I wanted to know _____ .

2. She remembered _____ .

3. We can't understand _____ .

4. Mary told me _____ .

5. Workers will have to learn _____ .

Match each word and phrase in Column A below with the item in Column B that has a similar meaning. Circle your answers.

A	B
1. around the clock	**a.** the shape of the watch
	b. avoid work
	c. day and night
2. up to six workers	**a.** more than six workers
	b. six or fewer workers
	c. fewer than six workers
3. will drop from 12 percent	**a.** will reach 12 percent
	b. will be above 12 percent
	c. will be below 12 percent
4. fourfold	**a.** four times
	b. a cloth with four corners
	c. a robot's name
5. undercutting American prices	**a.** charging the same as Americans
	b. charging less than Americans
	c. charging more than Americans
6. take time out	**a.** arrive late
	b. stop what they are doing
	c. move faster

Choose one of the phrases above and use it in a sentence.

Follow-up Activities

1. Choose one of the "New Occupations for the 1990s." Check the meaning of each occupational title. Then write a description of the job, telling what a person with that job would do. Use specific examples.

2. Choose one of the emerging careers listed below and ask a group of people what they think the job is. Compare your answers with those of other students.

house and pet sitter   cryogenic technician
aquaculturist   plant therapist
child advocate   shyness consultant
executive rehabilitative consultant

3. Find the article "Eight Scenarios for Work in the Future" in *The Futurist* (June 1983) and write a summary of one of the scenarios.

4. Read the comment below by a working mother. Find out how people feel about mothers who work from the time the children are born. What is their attitude toward day-care centers? Should fathers and mothers share the care of children?

> "We working mothers (especially the ones who would rather be with their children for a few years after they're born) are bitter. My present job is a good one — although it is clerical, it offers me a wider range of responsibilities than I've ever had in the past. However, no matter how good I've got at it, there isn't a day that goes by that I don't long to be with my child and watch her develop. I work on Capitol Hill and I strongly feel that at least the government should set up day-care centers for the children of working mothers."

Chapter Review

1. What do you think Jay Rohrlich's reaction would be to the values described in "A New Set of Work Values"?

2. To what extent do the jobs described in "Their Work Is Play" reflect the values in "A New Set of Work Values"?

3. Consider the following life cycle of John Smith. In what ways does his life differ from those of today? Would you like to have a similar life?

One of the Many Alternative Life Cycles the Future Might Offer

The Life of John Smith: 1985–2070

Birthplace: Chicago   *Status of Mother*: Single, Age 27

Age 1 year–   Attended elementary school.
8 years:

Age 8:   Traveled with a class of fifteen students. Visited a number of countries around the world. Learned several languages and cultures.

Age 10:   Returned to the United States and resumed formal studies.

Age 15:   Entered a rotating work-study program, electing to serve as an apprentice in three fields: architecture, social research, and communications science.

Age 18:   Went back to formal studies in the liberal arts. Also took advanced courses in architecture.

Age 19:   Spent three years abroad, studying comparative architecture.

Age 22:   Returned to the United States and was employed as a draftsman. Lived for two years in an urban commune with nine other young professionals.

Age 24:   Moved into an apartment with three friends — two female and one male. They were all "married" to each other, and all income and properties were pooled.

Age 27:   Divorced himself from his living arrangements and married a woman who was also divorced. She had one child, aged 6. Took and passed his architectural exams.

Age 35:   He and his wife took two-year leaves from their jobs, took their 14-year-old son and went to live on Nantucket. There, the three of them jointly developed their interests in the arts: painting, sketching, and sculpting.

Age 38:   Divorced his wife and lived by himself.

Age 50:   Set up house with two career women in their mid-forties. The relationship was economic and sexual, but not exclusive . . . he dated other women and they dated other men.

Age 60:   Left his job and residence, and went to teach communications science to students in a developing country.

Age 65:   Returned to the United States and resumed work part-time. Also went back to school part-time to update his formal education.

Age 67:   Remarried. His new wife had two children, both grown with children of their own.

Age 72:   Took a two-year leave and he, his wife, and one of their grandchildren traveled around the world. The 16-year-old grandchild remained with a family in London. He and his wife returned home.

Age 74:   Resumed work and school. Became interested in photography. Developed it as a full-time hobby and part-time income.

Age 80:   Took on a teaching position at a nearby university. His students ranged in age from 12 to 87. His topic was comparative architecture.

Age 85:   Died of sudden lung failure.

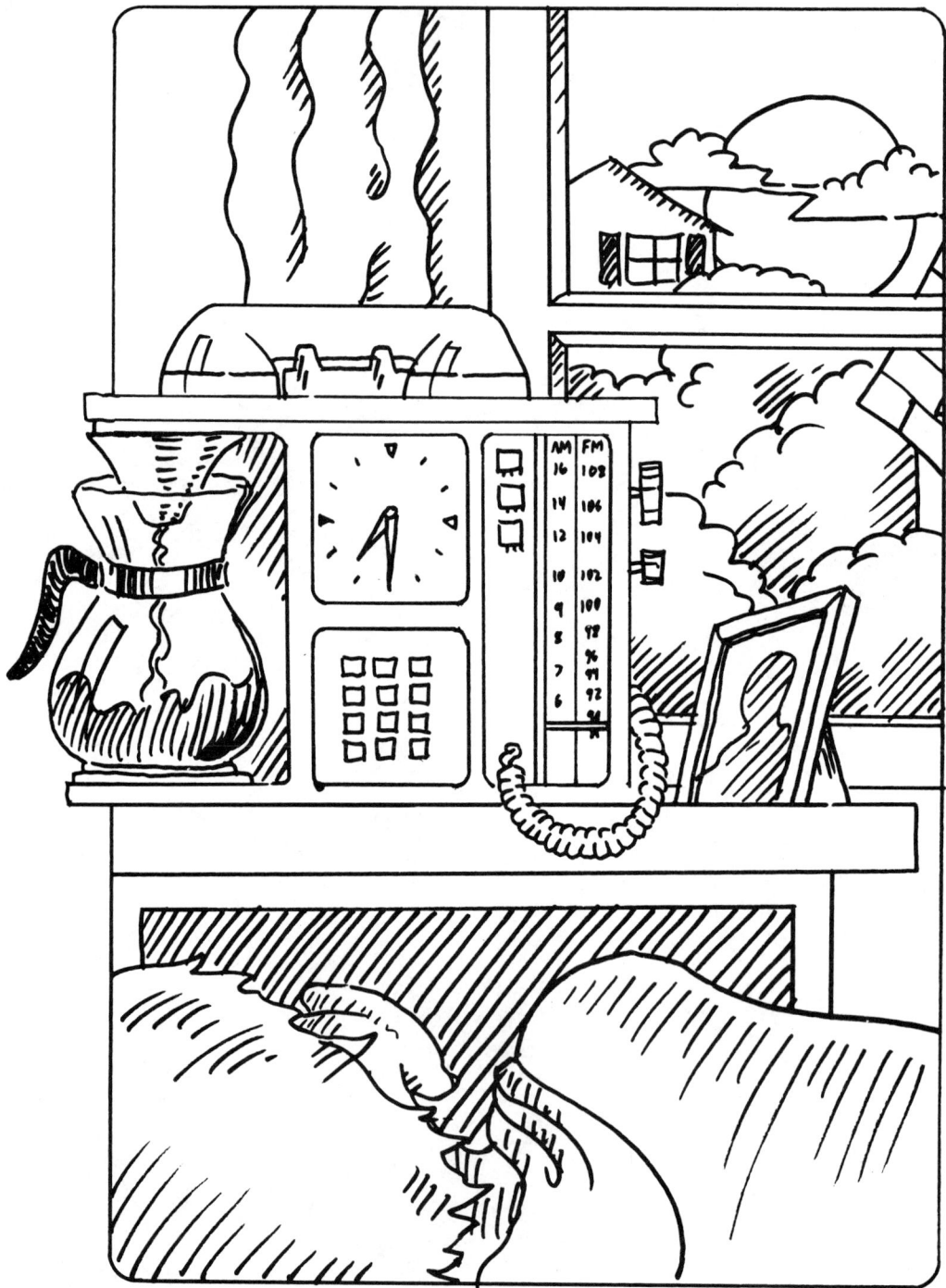

Modern Conveniences $\boxed{8}$

Airplanes, telephones, elevators, watches. These are some of the conveniences that make our world "modern." But how convenient are these conveniences? Do they have disadvantages as well as advantages? The authors in this chapter consider some aspects of these conveniences that we usually do not consider.

Chances Are You'll Wait

Before You Read

Newspaper articles provide us with a great variety of information from different sources. In this article from the *Los Angeles Times*, Lee Dembart summarizes and simplifies a report about waiting for an elevator that was originally published in *Mathematics Magazine*.

Think About It

How often do you use elevators? When do you take an elevator and when do you use the stairs?

Are there any things you like or dislike about elevators?

Chances Are You'll Wait

Lee Dembart

1   One of the complications of modern life is that when you're waiting for an up elevator, the first one to arrive is usually going down and when you're waiting for a down elevator, the first one to arrive is usually going up. This observation, gleaned from years of waiting for elevators, turns out to be true for reasons built into the laws of nature, according to the author of an article in *Mathematics Magazine*.

2   Why is the first elevator usually going in the wrong direction? The answer, according to A. Wuffle, the pen name used by a professor of political science and social psychology at the University of California, Irvine, is relatively simple: In most buildings, when you're on a low floor, the chances are that you probably want to go up because there are more possible destinations above you than below you. However, there are also probably more elevators above you than below you, which means that when they reach you, they will be doing down. Similarly, when you're on a high floor, you probably want to go down, but because there are more elevators below you, when they get to you they are going up.

3   This analysis does not apply to the first floor or to the top floor of a building. All elevators at the first floor go up, and all elevators at the top floor go down. Of course, as any elevator rider will attest, you will still probably have to wait a long time for one. During the morning rush hour, most people want to go up, and during the evening rush hours, most people want to go down. Nonetheless, Wuffle said in an interview, "The general conclusion is still correct."

4   There are psychological factors at work in our perceptions of elevators as well. Since negative emotions are felt more acutely than positive ones, we tend to remember our disappointments with elevators more keenly than we remember our satisfactions. We forget the times that the right elevator came and focus on the times that it didn't.

Comprehenion

Expand your understanding of the article's main ideas.

1.   Elevators always seem to be going in the wrong direction when we are waiting for one. Is this because of poor building design, natural reasons, or too many people in the buildings?

2.   Why doesn't Wuffle's analysis apply to the top and bottom floors?

3. According to the article, which of the following situations is most likely to occur?

   a. Your chances of getting an elevator going in your direction are better when you are going up than when you are going down.

   b. Your chances of getting an elevator that is going up are better in the morning than in the evening.

   c. The chances that the first elevator that comes along will be going in your direction are not good.

Applications

Relate the article to events in your own life.

1. Name some advantages and disadvantages of modern buildings.

2. Do you agree that negative emotions are felt more strongly than positive emotions? Can you think of examples?

3. Waiting can be frustrating. Besides elevators, what are some other things for which we often have to wait? Why don't we usually like to wait?

4. Is waiting always negative? Can you think of any advantages to waiting?

Telephones

Before You Read

Penny Ward Moser wrote this article about telephones for the magazine *Discover*, which emphasizes science and technology. She shows her enthusiasm for the new telephone technology and describes what she discovered about it. In the selection that follows, she tells about an exhibit of the new phones.

Think About It

What kinds of telephones are most popular in your country now?

What kind of telephone would you like to have? What would you expect it to do for you?

Telephones

Penny Ward Moser

1 The show had hundreds of exhibits, including computer switches galore — switches you could sit in, switches you could walk through. There was even a switch wearing jungle camouflage. Then there were the phones. Not necessarily the phones of war, but the phones of today's desktops. One office phone had 350 features. Another told you who was calling before you picked it up; if you didn't want to talk to that person, you could have your phone tell a white lie to the other phone, which would repeat it to the caller. All the action takes place on a little liquid-crystal display screen on the phone. (You punch in your little white lie beforehand.) This same system gives certain phones rank and privilege. If your boss wants to call you and your line is busy, his phone will tell your phone to let you know that you're about to be "overridden," and your phone will beep and the screen will say "override" and you have five seconds to tell your party that he's going on automatic hold.

2 One phone could actually talk to me. The man demonstrating it pushed a few buttons and I put it to my ear. Suddenly, his phone back in Virginia was talking to him about his messages. It had one of those little synthesized voices — friendly and helpful. It could repeat a taped message, store it, erase it. It hadn't made any mistakes. "This could replace a switchboard operator," I said. "That's exactly what it does," he replied.

3 I discovered phones that can recognize your voice (voice recognition) and be activated by it (voice activation). You can teach them to recognize your pronunciation of all ten numbers. Then you just yell: "Hey, phone" (or any other voice code you pick), pause, "five-five-five, one-eight-six-four." And the number will ring. For those in a hurry there is a phone that will let you program the numbers and code them to a person's name. So all you have to do is yell "Hey, phone," pause, "Grandma." And Granny will be on the line.

4 If Granny is old and feeble, she can wear her phone's remote monitor, a device about the size of a beeper; by pushing a button on it, she can signal her phone to call for help. If she falls down out in the yard, she can push the button, and the phone's little voice will call a rescue squad, or a neighbor — whoever is programmed in — and say "medical emergency at . . ."

5 Another phone gives you a discriminating unlisted number. When someone calls you, a little voice interrupts and asks the caller for your three-digit code — in effect, a secret password. The caller then punches in the code on a Touch-Tone phone, or if at a dial phone, says it, and the call goes through. If the caller doesn't know the code, the phone takes a message. "It screens out those telephone marketing calls," one phone expert told me. "You know, those little voice-synthesized advertising messages that come from other machines. It's machine wars."

6   As I learned more I realized that the telephone is going to change our day-to-day lives more than we think. Soon it and its accessories will become almost like one of the family. "Our phone will no longer be passive," John Peers, one of the optimistic entrepreneurs of the new industry, explained to me. "It will be active."

7   Very active, if Peers's efforts bear fruit. He is the president of Androbot, a California robot manufacturing firm, and is working on something he calls synthetic animals, or "mechanimals." A mechanimal, which Peers thinks will be in the trial stage in a year or so, will combine the telephone with tiny topographical robots (ones that can scuttle around like small R2-D2s). "After all," he says, "when the phone rings, why should you get up to answer it? Why not just have it come to you?"

8   The mechanimal in your home will always know where you are, because it detects your body heat with infrared sensors. When the phone rings, it hurries over to you. If there are two people in the room, it stops and its synthesized voice says, "I' ringing." Since it is programmed to respond to your voice commands, you say "Come here." And it obeys. That's just the beginning. The mechanimal will be able to sense smoke in the house and alert you to a fire. It could hear a pipe burst during the night or let you know that someone was breaking in. "Eventually," Peers says, "your mechanimal will be able to stand by the foot of your bed, monitor your breathing and your pulse rate, and try to wake you if something goes wrong. If you don't respond, it will call for help."

9   The General Electric HomeMinder is another faithful telephone-operated servant. With one end plugged into a phone jack and the other into your household wiring, the HomeMinder can do little chores — in fact, a hundred of them — while you're out. You simply plug a light or an appliance into a special module, then plug that into an electrical socket. Signals from the HomeMinder flow through your household circuit, activating whatever modules you choose. You can call from any Touch-Tone phone in the country (or use a hand-held tone generator on a dial phone) and turn on your lights, switch on your stereo, warm up your Jacuzzi, start your air conditioner or even your bug zapper if you're going to have a barbecue. You can program it to do the same thing everyday, or if you're doing to be away, to turn on various appliances at random so that your house looks lived in.

10   Talking telephones may be next — and they will certainly be more useful. John Peers of Androbot feels we're fast approaching the day when the telephone and add-ons will be able to talk to us and to each other. Some already do. "When you can talk to your telephone, and your telephone can talk to other telephones, you'll have access to your dialogue [talking] computer," says Peers. "You'll be able to turn around and ask your telephone a question: it will call another phone and ask it to ask its computer, and then it will get back to your phone, which will get back to you. You don't need to be near the computer. You don't need to be near the screen. You do need to be near the telephone."

11   If your home phone were there to greet you when you came in the door, gave you your messages, had started dinner, and asked you how your day was, then stayed by your bed at night to guard you, how long would it be before you named it? Before it became sort of a person? Maybe your best friend?

12   I used to be afraid of all this, but now I'm not. I still respect my old phone at home, but I love my new phone at work. I'm not unusual, one technology expert has told me. I'm in what they call a "phase shift." Something I'd become accustomed to is changing forever. In this case it's the telephone. The telephone is becoming almost alive.

Comprehension

1. What are some things that the phones at the communication show can do?

2. Some phones can recognize a voice. How do you activate these phones?

3. How can some of these phones be very helpful to old people?

4. What will a mechanimal be able to do?

5. What is the author's attitude toward the new phones?

Discussion

1. How often do you use telephones?

2. What uses do you have for telephones?

3. How have telephones affected our way of life? What did people do before they had phones?

Language Practice

Find the meaning of the underlined words below. Then rewrite each sentence, substituting appropriate words or phrases for the underlined ones.

1. It could repeat a taped message, store it, erase it. (See paragraph 2.)

_____

_____

2. It hadn't made any <u>mistakes</u>. (See paragraph 2.)

   _____

3. So all you have to do is <u>yell</u>, "Hey, phone," <u>pause</u>, "Grandma." (See paragraph 3.)

   _____

4. A mechanimal, which Peers thinks will be in the trial <u>stage</u> in a year or so, will combine the telephone with <u>tiny</u> topographical robots. (See paragraph 7.)

   _____

   _____

   _____

5. It is programmed to <u>respond</u> to your voice commands. (See paragraph 8.)

   _____

6. The mechanimal will be able to <u>alert you to a fire</u>. (See paragraph 8.)

   _____

7. Something I'd become <u>accustomed to</u> is changing forever. (See paragraph 11.)

   _____

8. You can teach a telephone to <u>recognize</u> your voice. (See paragraph 3.)

   _____

Rewrite the sentences below, substituting words from the following list for the underlined phrases.

bear fruit	scuttle around
is completed	there is a problem
keeps away	

1. It <u>screens out</u> those telephone marketing calls.

   _____

2. If you punch in the code, the call <u>goes through</u>.

   _____

3. The efforts of the inventor may <u>produce good results</u>.

   _____

4. The little robots will be able to <u>move around quickly</u>.

   _____

5. The robot will wake you if <u>something goes wrong</u>.

   _____

Fill in the blanks in the sentences below with words from this list:

alert	erase	obey	replace
detect	interrupt	program	

1. If Grandma is out in the yard and falls down, she can _____ her neighbors by pushing the button on her remote monitor.

2. If there is a fire in your house, the robot can _____ smoke and ring a bell.

3. You can _____ a telephone so that it will respond to your voice.

4. When you are talking on the phone and someone else calls you, a little voice could _____ your conversation and say, "Excuse me, you have another call."

5. It's possible that if you push the wrong button, you will _____ all the messages on the tape.

Write six sentences. In each sentence, use a verb and a noun from the following list.

Verbs	Nouns
tape	message
store	code
erase	calls
punch in	numbers
push	robot
program	buttons

1. _____

2. _____

3. _____

4. _____

5. _____

6. _____

The sentences below are not in correct order. Reorder them to show how the ideas are connected to each other. Write the number 1 beside the sentence that you think should be first, the number 2 beside the sentence that you think should be second, and so on.

_____ You can call home from any phone in the country and turn on the light in your home.

_____ You plug one end into the phone and the other into your household wiring.

_____ The HomeMinder is another useful servant that is operated through the telephone.

_____ So signals from the HomeMinder can move through your household and activate whatever you choose.

_____ Or you can program the HomeMinder to turn on the heat at the same time every day.

In the article we find: "When the phone rings, why should you get up to answer it?" On the lines below, use that sentence pattern to comment on other kinds of experiences.

EXAMPLE: If he is not hungry, why should he eat?

1. _____

2. _____

3. _____

On the lines below, write a paragraph about a device, answering the following questions. Use paragraph 3 of the reading as a model.

1. What is the purpose of the device?

2. How does the device work?

3. Give an example of how it works.

_____

_____

_____

_____

Complete the following paragraph in three or four sentences.

I used to be afraid of (something), but now I'm not. _____

_____

_____

_____

_____

Complete the following paragraph in three or four sentences.

Something I'd become accustomed to is changing forever. _____

_____

_____

_____

Follow-up Activities

1. Consult your classmates and list the things they wrote about in the exercise above ("Something I'd become accustomed to is changing forever").

2. If you had a mechanimal in your house, what commands would you program it to respond to? List some commands and compare your list with those of other students.

3. A telephone may have many accessories; for example, a device that interrupts a call with a little beep to tell you someone else is calling you. Talk to people or look in magazines to identify some accessories available with automobiles, vacuum cleaners, computers, and so on. Choose one device or machine and list its accessories.

4. People and things may seem active or passive to us. A telephone that we dial may seem passive; a telephone that talks to us may seem active. Choose a person, group, or device that seems active or passive to you. Be prepared to give examples of how the person or thing is active or passive.

5. The article describes various advantages of the new phone and the mechanimal. Survey your friends or classmates to find out what they consider some possible disadvantages of these devices. Report your results to the class.

6. Look up the article "Telecommuters" in *The Futurist* (June 1983) and be prepared to report on it.

Topics for Further Discussion or Writing

1. In many countries there are public phone booths. But each year there seem to be fewer and fewer phone booths. Why are they disappearing? What is replacing them?

2. The method of making a public telephone call may differ from place to place. Learn about and describe some of these differences.

3. Pretend that you are calling a friend to invite him or her to the movies. Write a dialogue and compare it with those of other students.

4. The cost of making long-distance telephone calls varies. Find out the costs of making calls between two countries. Then tell what are the best and the worst times to call. Why?

5. How important is it to have a telephone? How does that importance vary for different people?

Watches for Our Time

Before You Read

In this newspaper column, Diane White writes about one of the complexities of modern life: the many choices we have when we want to buy a manufactured product.

Think About It

What kind of watch do you have? Does it give you any information in addition to the time?

Have you bought a gift for someone recently? Did you have to choose from many items when you bought the gift? Do you like to go shopping and make choices?

Watches for Our Time

Diane White

1 I wanted a watch. Nothing fancy. Just a basic watch.

2   "What will you be using it for?" the saleswoman asked.

3   "Well," I said, "I was hoping to be able to tell the time."

4   She laughed, a bit hard, I thought, considering nobody had said anything funny.

5   "Naturally all our models come equipped with a basic timekeeping mode," she said. "But what else did you want it for?"

6   I tried to imagine something else I might want to do with a watch. All I could think of was that I might wear it in the shower by mistake. "Waterproof," I said. "I want one that's waterproof."

7   She reached into the case and took out something roughly the size of Big Ben. "This is our professional diver's watch," she said. "Water-tested to 600 feet, or 200 meters, below sea level."

8   I tried to visualize an occasion when I might be 600 feet below sea level. Perhaps if I went on a cruise and the ship sank. But if that happened, why would I need to know the time?

9   "It's digital, as you can see," she said, "and luminous, mar-resistant, railroad-approved. It has a bilingual English-Spanish calendar, count-down alarm, pressure-vented strap . . ."

10   I broke in. "Actually," I said, "I don't plan to be spending that much time under water."

11   She seemed disappointed.

12   "Perhaps, then," she said, "you'd like something dressy."

13   She took out a tray full of jewel-encrusted golden wafers and held one up to the light. "This watch is so thin," she said, "that when I turn it sideways it actually seems to disappear."

14   As fascinated as I was by the idea of owning a disappearing watch, it seemed a bit impractical. I told her I wanted something a little sturdier, a watch I could wear to work.

15   "The busy executive!" she cried, mistaking me for someone else. "Say no more. This is what you've been looking for."

16   It was a combination digital watch and minicomputer. She touched a button, and it sprang into action, reeling off the times in 23 world capitals. She pressed another button and an alarm played "Boogie Woogie Bugle Boy." You could leave yourself reminders on the computer and, at the appointed time, a message and a picture would appear on the face. A little telephone, for example, with the words, "Call Mom." Or a tiny plane and the message "Fly N.Y."

17   I told her I wasn't sure I could live with a watch that was obviously smarter than I am. She showed me a few more: A runner's watch that nags you by beeping when you don't keep up the pace. A watch with a tachymeter for yachting and a tachometer for auto racing. A watch that plays blackjack. Another that analyzes the performance of stocks or thoroughbreds, depending on your interests. Yet another that traces the phases of the moon, charts biorhythms, compiles astrological profiles and has a monthly alarm that plays the cavalry charge at the exact moment you're most likely to conceive.

18   None of them seemed right.

19   I finally found the watch I wanted, on the back of a cereal box. I sent in the boxtop and a modest check. Back it came in the mail. Tom Mix points his little six-shooters at the numbers. He looks pretty funny when it gets to be about 9:45. I have to wind it every day. And I've got all this Hot Ralston to eat. But I don't care. All my watch does is tell the time. What more could I ask for?

Comprehension

1. Why didn't White like the watches that the saleswoman showed her?

2. What uses did White imagine for a waterproof watch? Can you think of other uses?

3. How do we know that this article is humorous? What is the first sentence that made you think it was funny?

4. What is the main point of the article?

5. The title of the article can have two meanings. What are they?

Discussion

1. What are some other common devices that have become complicated? You might consider some things usually found in kitchens or cars.

2. What are some devices with combined functions that you find useful?

3. What are some devices with combined functions that you think are useless?

Language Practice

Find the meaning of the underlined words in the following sentences. Then rewrite each sentence, substituting appropriate words or phrases for the underlined ones.

1. She took out something <u>roughly</u> the size of Big Ben. (See paragraph 7.)

    _____

2. I tried to <u>visualize the occasion</u> when I might be 600 feet below sea level. (See paragraph 8.)

    _____

    _____

3. Perhaps if I went on a <u>cruise</u> and the ship sank. (See paragraph 8.)

    _____

4. The watch <u>seemed impractical</u>. (See paragraph 14.) _____

5. <u>Say no more</u>. (See paragraph 15.) _____

The words <u>a bit</u> and <u>a little</u> can describe adjectives.

1. Below list the three adjectives in this article that are preceded by these phrases.

_____ _____ _____

2. Write a sentence using one of the phrases.

_____

_____

The sentences below are not in correct order. Write them in the correct order, adding words or phrases from this list to make the transition from one sentence to the next clearer.

as a result   on the other hand
for example   similarly

If you have to wake up at 6:00 A.M., at that time the watch will play a song or start beeping.
They may be very difficult to repair.
There are now watches that work as computers.
If you have a doctor's appointment at 3:00 P.M., the watch will beep at 3:00 and the word "doctor" will appear on the face of the watch.
Computer watches can be too complicated.
They allow you to leave messages that will remind you of something.

_____

_____

_____

_____

_____

_____

Write a paragraph about something you bought recently by answering the following questions.

1. What did you want? _____

2. What did you want to use it for? _____

3. Where did you get it? _____

4. What kinds were there? _____

5. Which one did you get? _____

6. Why? _____

Fill in the blanks below with your own words and phrases.

I needed a(n) _____ so I looked in the newspaper.

There I found _____ . The advertisement showed

_____ . The one that I liked best _____ .

As a result, I _____ .

Complete this sentence with your own ideas.

She (or he) seemed disappointed because _____

_____ .

Complete this paragraph with your own ideas.

There are two kinds of _____ . _____

_____

_____ .

I like the _____ better because _____

_____ .

"If I went on a cruise, the ship might sink." This word pattern refers to a possible action and a possible result. Write three sentences below using this pattern.

EXAMPLE: If I went to the library, I might learn something.

1. _____

2. _____

3. _____

Complete this dialogue with your own ideas.

Customer:	I'd like _____ .
Salesperson:	What kind _____ ?
Customer:	_____ .
Salesperson:	Don't you want _____ ?
Customer:	No, because _____ .

Follow-up Activities

1. For each word or phrase below, list some examples on the lines provided.

    a. Models of cars (or of something else) _____

    _____

    _____

    b. Impractical gifts _____

    _____

    _____

    c. Things that look funny _____

    _____

    _____

    d. Times when someone nagged you _____

    _____

    _____

e. Things you did by mistake _____

_____

_____

2. Read the back of a cereal box. What information did you find there? Compare your information with that found by other students. Which box was the most interesting?

3. Choose one of the items listed below and find out if different kinds are available (from a store or advertisements). Compare your research with that of other students. Decide which kinds are most popular in the class. You may add other items to the list.

hamburgers   TV sets   thermometers   cereals

4. On the lines below, describe the differences between these pictures.

_____

_____

_____

5. Fill in the blanks below with words that have the same meaning as the following phrases. When you complete the puzzle, read the first letters of the words from top to bottom. They should make a word that means strong.

___ ___ ___   a pronoun that refers to a female

___ ___ ___ ___   people who sell watches depend on it

___ ___ ___ ___ ___   the opposite of <u>over</u>

___ ___ ___ ___ ___ ___   somebody who runs a lot

___ ___ ___ ___ ___   somebody who is underwater a lot

___ ___ ___ ___ ___   a fancy boat

_____

Airlines

Before You Read

Here Andy Rooney, a TV commentator, notes some things that airlines do well and then complains about things that they don't do well. The article is written in the form of a letter of advice to the airlines.

Think About It

If you enjoy airline trips, what do you like about them?

What don't you like about airline trips?

Airlines

Andy Rooney

1 Although no airline has ever written to me asking for advice, I'm going to give them some while a cross-country flight I just made is fresh in my mind.

2 The good thing you have going for you, airlines, is that we are all somewhat exhilarated by the thought of going to a distant place. I'm not a chronic airline knocker, but getting there these days is too often an unpleasant experience and, for your own good, I don't want you to take the magic out of it.

3 You do a lot of things well. You seem to try hard. I like the way

one airline will give us information about another over the phone or at the counter, even when there's no business in it for them. Your facilities are usually clean and your employees courteous, but there are some things I want to talk to you about.

4   You seem to understand that all of us hate standing in line at the ticket counter at the airport, for example, but what you don't seem to realize is that we wouldn't hate it so much if we were absolutely sure we were standing in the right line and that it was necessary for us to stand in it at all. Which line is which? Can we go directly to the gate? Are we really checked in? You aren't going to give our seat away, are you? Which one of all these sheets of paper in this envelope is really the ticket? How many times do we have to show things to people before we get on the plane, and whom do we have to show what to? Help us with these matters.

5   It's a good feeling once we are actually on board and seated, but it takes too long to get there. It takes too long to get off, too. Couldn't you board and unload through two doors?

6   One of the reasons it's taking too long is that you're letting people carry too much junk on board. They take junk on board because it is still taking too long to retrieve a bag that's been checked through.

7   I was in Los Angeles last week and the return flight to New York was one hour and fifty-five minutes late taking off. I don't know why you didn't give us any explanation, but as soon as we got in the air the pilot came on and thanked us for our patience and understanding. I had not been patient and understanding at all, and I resent the pilot's assumption I was. As a matter of fact, I was damned *impatient,* if the pilot wants to know the truth.

8   There's something else I want to tell you about your pilots, too. Most of us hate the folksy ones. One of the best ways to pass time in flight is by sleeping. Last week, about half an hour out of Los Angeles, I was sound asleep and blissfully unaware of the discomforts of a crowded flight when the pilot blasted me awake over the intercom.

9   "There's a good view of the crater formed when that meteorite hit the Earth near Winslow, Arizona, over there to our right, ladies and gentlemen. The walls of the crater are 525 feet high."

10   Thanks a lot, Captain. I happen to be on the *left* side of the plane and can't see a thing. Where were you when we wanted to know why our flight was two hours late? Not only that, you told me to buckle my seat belt for my own comfort and convenience. I happen to think you wanted me to keep it buckled for *your* convenience, so I wouldn't stand up and get in the stewardesses' way. But that's another story. So what am I supposed to do? Get up and lean over someone on the right side of the plane or try to go back to sleep?

11   I can't complain much about your stewardesses. They aren't as young or as pretty as they used to be and this seems like a step in the right direction, but I do have one or two suggestions. Will you please tell them to stop making that announcement where they say, "If there's

anything we can do to make your flight more enjoyable, please don't hesitate to call on us."

12   The chances are she's got a planeload of people and we'll all be lucky if she has time to throw lunch at us. We've got about as much chance of getting special attention from a stewardess as we'd have getting the only floor nurse in the middle of the night in a crowded hospital.

13   And another thing. Stop having her ask us if we want cream in our coffee. I don't know whether you airlines have noticed or not, but none of you serve cream anymore. You serve a white liquid plastic for the coffee.

14   You notice I haven't complained about your food. Actually I feel sorry for the chefs who design and prepare your meals. It is obvious they start with good ingredients and do well by them in the kitchen, but bricks wouldn't stand up to what happens to airline food between the hangar where it's fixed and the passenger's tray table. So, a last bit of advice. Keep the food simple. Don't try to serve us scrambled eggs on a flaming sword.

Comprehension

1.   What are two things that Rooney likes about airlines?

2.   What are two things that Rooney doesn't like about airlines?

3.   What is Rooney's suggestion to speed up airline boarding?

4.   What kind of pilots does Rooney complain about?

5.   What does Rooney think about the airlines' coffee?

Discussion

1.   How would you rate airlines in comparison to other forms of transportation?

2.   Have you found any differences among airlines?

3.   What is one piece of advice that you would like to give to airlines?

Language Practice

Find the meaning of the underlined words in the following sentences. Then rewrite each sentence using words with similar meanings.

1. I'm not a <u>chronic</u> airline <u>knocker</u>. (See paragraph 2.)

   _____

2. The flight is <u>fresh</u> in my mind. (See paragraph 1.)

   _____

Read: "I had not been patient and understanding and I resent the pilot's assumption that I was."

1. How does the writer feel toward the pilot here?

   _____

2. What did the pilot assume?

   _____

When you get something back (such as your suitcase at the airport), you *retrieve* it. What else could you retrieve? List some items below. If you can't think of anything, ask someone who works with a computer.

_____   _____   _____   _____

Saying something *ironic* means saying something that is the opposite of what you mean. Which phrase in paragraph 10 is ironic? Write it below.

_____

Pretend that you work for an airline. Answer four of the questions that Rooney asks in paragraph 4. Write both questions and answers on the appropriate lines below.

1. Question: _____

   Answer: _____

2. Question: _____

   Answer: _____

3. Question: _____

 Answer: _____

4. Question: _____

 Answer: _____

Pretend that you are at an airport. Make up a question about each of the following and write them below.

1. your ticket _____

2. the time of departure _____

3. your baggage _____

Pretend that you are on an airplane. Ask the flight attendant for something (food, something to read, information about the arrival time, and so on). Below write a four-line dialogue between you and the flight attendant.

You: _____

Flight attendant: _____

You: _____

Flight attendant: _____

How do you spend your time at an airport, bus terminal, or railroad station while you are waiting to leave? Write your answer in two or three sentences below.

_____

_____

_____

_____

Write two or three sentences that describe what you would like airlines to do. Begin with "I would like . . ."

_____

_____

_____

The author uses words that describe positive and negative experiences:

Positive   **Negative**

clean _____   unpleasant _____

courteous _____   impatient _____

patience _____   discomfort _____

convenience _____   hate _____

1. Next to each word above, write a word that is opposite in meaning.

2. Describe one of your travel experiences, using as many of the above words as you can. Write three or four sentences.

_____

_____

_____

_____

Write a four- or five-sentence paragraph that describes the worst or the best thing that ever happened to you on a trip. Make up a title for your paragraph.

_____

_____

_____

_____

_____

Follow-up Activities

1. Ask people how they pass the time when they are on or waiting for public transportation. Compare your results with those of other students.

2. *Facilities* is a general term meaning help that makes things convenient for us.

   a. List the facilities at an airport:

   _____   _____   _____

   _____   _____   _____

   b. List the facilities at a school that you know:

   _____   _____   _____

   _____   _____   _____

   c. What facilities are necessary for a school sports program? List them below.

   _____   _____   _____

   _____   _____   _____

   Compare your lists with those of other students.

3. Prepare a questionnaire on airline service. Write questions about the food, the flight attendants, the lines, the announcements, the departures, and so on. Combine your questions with those of other students to make one good questionnaire. Have people answer the questionnaire and summarize the results.

Chapter Review

1. The authors in this chapter have different attitudes toward aspects of today's technology. Choose two of the authors and compare their attitudes. Be sure you have examples to support your points.

2. The results of modern technology often cause problems when we try to assimilate them into traditional cultures. In some skyscrapers, for example, there is no thirteenth floor because thirteen is considered an unlucky number. In some places, people are not supposed to turn on the electricity on a rest day because making light is considered work. Do you know of other examples that illustrate the difficulties some cultures are having as they adapt to or reject modern conveniences?

3. One reading concerns a watch and another a telephone. What uses can you think of for a watch-telephone?

Challenges

9

This last chapter presents a set of topics that concern all of us: poverty; the effect of population increases; the attitudes of young people toward their future; the danger of nuclear power.

Seven Signs of Change

Before You Read

Much information is presented nowadays in the form of charts. This selection, which we call "Databank," consists entirely of charts giving data on contemporary families.

Think About It

What kind of information is presented in charts?

What are some different types of families?

Databank: Seven Signs of Change

Larry Greiner

Types of Households
(As a percentage of all households)

Nonfamily Households	18.8% / 26.8%
Family Households	81.2% / 73.2%
Married Couple Fam.	70.5% / 59.5%
Male Householder Fam.	1.9% / 2.4%
Female Householder Fam.	8.7% / 11.3%

1970 ▢ ▨ 1983

Nonfamily Household: Contains a person living alone or with non-relatives.

Family Household: Contains a householder—a dwelling's renter or owner—and at least one other person related to the householder by birth, marriage, or adoption. The U.S. groups family households as: (1) Married-Couple Households, (2) Male-Householder Households (No Wife Present), and (3) Female-Householder Households (No Husband Present).

Married Couples Run Most Families
(Percent of all families in each group, both partners present, in 1984. With or without children.)

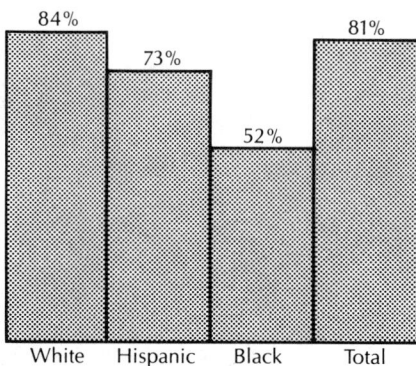

White	Hispanic	Black	Total
84%	73%	52%	81%

The Family Shrinks
(Average family size)

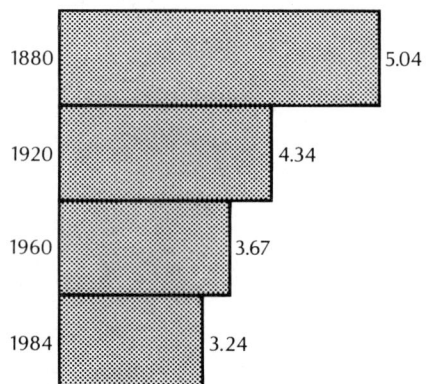

1880	5.04
1920	4.34
1960	3.67
1984	3.24

Graphic Chart & Map 1986

Children Live in Many Types of Families
(Children under 18, in 1982)

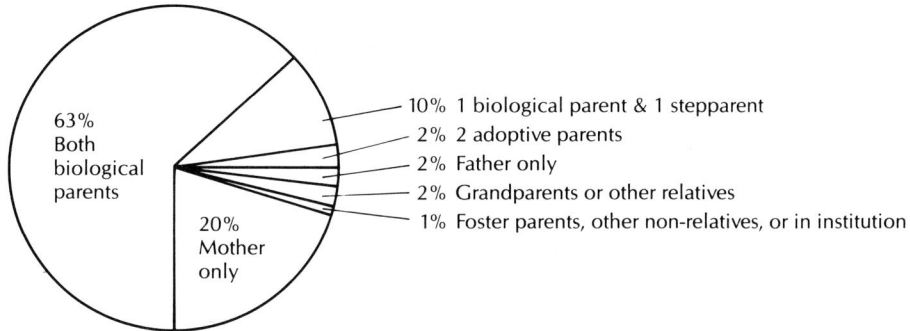

63%
Both
biological
parents

20%
Mother
only

— 10% 1 biological parent & 1 stepparent
— 2% 2 adoptive parents
— 2% Father only
— 2% Grandparents or other relatives
— 1% Foster parents, other non-relatives, or in institution

Women Support More Families Alone
(Families maintained by women, with and without children under 18, as a percentage of all families)

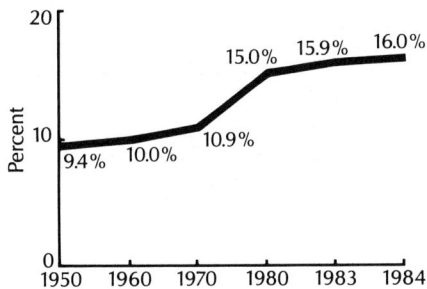

20

Percent

10

0

9.4% 10.0% 10.9% 15.0% 15.9% 16.0%

1950 1960 1970 1980 1983 1984

A Second Paycheck Lures More Mothers Outside the Home
(Percentage of married women with children under 18 and husbands present who hold full-time jobs outside the home.)

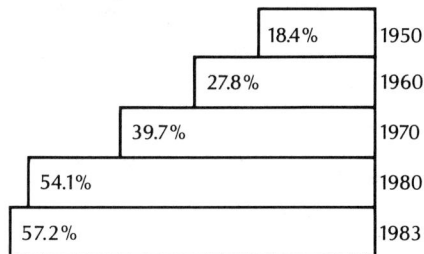

18.4%		1950
27.8%		1960
39.7%		1970
54.1%		1980
57.2%		1983

Poverty Grips Many Families
(Families in each group with incomes below the poverty level.*)

	All Races	White	Black	Hispanic
1959:	18.5%	15.2%	48.1%	NA
1980:	10.3%	8.0%	28.9%	23.2%
1983:	12.3%	9.7%	32.4%	26.1%

* The level varies from year to year. In 1983, the U.S. government defined a family of four as poor if its income was below $10,178. NA: Not available.

Comprehension

Expand your understanding of the charts' information.

1. If the only members of a family were a girl and her uncle, that family would be classified here as

    a. a nonfamily household

    b. a male-householder household

    c. a female-householder household

2. From 1970 to 1983, what trend do you see in types of households?

3. Which of the following is true?

    a. Forty-eight percent of black families are not run by married couples.

    b. In 1982, 40 percent of all children lived in homes with only one adult.

    c. The percentage of married women who have full-time jobs outside the home increased by 12 percent from 1960 to 1980.

4. Statistics can be misleading. Look at the chart on poverty. It's possible that the number of poor people increased between 1980 and 1983, but there is also another possibility. What is it?

5. In what decade was there a significant increase in the number of women who support families alone?

6. Using the charts as your information source, how would you describe a typical white family in 1983?

Applications

Relate the charts' information to your own experiences.

1. On the basis of the charts, describe the changes that are affecting women in the United States.

2. Write a summary (one or two sentences) that describes the typical family discussed in question 6 above.

3. Choose one category in the charts. What do you think the chart would look like if it described the same category in your country?

4. Choose one chart and write a two- or three-sentence summary of the information there.

5. Why do you think the changes described in the charts happened?

6. Use this information to make a chart:

Persons in Households	1980	Percent	1970	Percent
All Households	80,433,749	100.0	63,637,721	100.0
1 Person	18,222,236	22.7	11,157,804	17.5
2 Persons	25,151,422	31.3	18,769,652	29.5
3 Persons	13,962,220	17.4	10,908,899	17.1
4 Persons	12,398,290	15.4	9,847,770	15.5
5 Persons	6,227,664	7.7	6,244,710	9.8
6 or More Persons	4,471,917	5.6	6,708,886	10.5

It's Time to Rethink Population Policies

Before You Read

Dr. Lester Brown is the head of the Worldwatch Institute, a research group in Washington, D.C. He has written many books on world resources and population. In this selection, he discusses government population policies in some Third World countries.

Think About It

What are some characteristics of Third World countries?

What is "zero population growth"?

It's Time to Rethink Population Policies

Lester R. Brown

1 The past year has seen economies unravel in more and more Third World countries. In these poorest of nations, the struggle to maintain living standards may require governments to completely rethink their population policies.

2 Third World governments have two choices, it seems to me. They can act quickly to curb population growth, or they can wait until the pressure of population becomes so explosive that they must take harsh measures.

3   A shift in the Third World's prospects has come after a generation of economic growth that easily outpaced population growth. For many countries, this margin of safety has suddenly disappeared.

4   During the four years since the second oil price hike of 1979, world economic growth averaged 1.7 percent a year — exactly the same as population growth. The 1980s will be marked by continued high energy prices, broad deterioration of croplands and forests, burdensome debt in many Third World countries, and high interest rates assured by massive U.S. budget deficits. Together, these trends suggest that the world economy will be hard-pressed to expand by much more than 2 percent a year for the rest of the decade.

WIDENING GAP

5 For countries that have reached "zero population growth," such as West Germany, Belgium, or Hungary, a 2 percent annual growth in their economies will raise incomes a comfortable 2 percent each year. But in countries such as Kenya, Pakistan, or Ecuador, populations expand at 3 percent or more each year. There, economic growth of 2 percent will yield a steady *decline* in income and living standards.

6   For some, the slide has already begun. The World Bank reports that, in some 18 countries, most of them in Africa, incomes fell during the 1970s. Other African countries joined the list during the early 1980s.

7   The Inter-American Development Bank reported more bad news. In Latin America, per capita incomes in 1983 were 10 percent below those of 1980. If rapid population growth continues, many Latin American nations may end the '80s with incomes below those they began with.

8   In Africa, the decline in per capita income is closely tied to the decline in food production per person — a decline of 1 percent a year since 1970. Africa's rate of growth in food production, 2 percent a year, is quite respectable by international standards. But, lagging behind population growth of 3 percent a year — the fastest of any continent in history — Africa's growing food output really means increasingly less food per person.

CHINA'S EXAMPLE

9 Against this economic backdrop, Third World leaders are beginning to re-examine population policy. China was among the first countries to do so. In the late 1970s, Chinese leaders projected the nation's future population growth on the assumption that every couple would have two children. Their projection revealed that even with two-child families, China's population of 1 billion would grow another 300 to 400 million before stopping. They figured, further, that the future availability of cropland, water, energy, and jobs wouldn't support this growth without risking the past generation's hard-earned gains in living standards. So the leaders concluded that they had no choice but to press for one-child families.

10   In the West, we tend to shrink from the notion of a one-child family program sponsored by a government. But before condemning this demanding initiative, we need to consider that, for many countries, the only alternative is a rate of population growth that undermines living conditions. That alternative is all too visible in Africa today.

11   There are many differences between China and other densely populated developing countries such as Bangladesh, India, Egypt, Nigeria, or Mexico. But the principal difference may be that the Chinese have had the foresight to make projections of their population and resources, and the courage to translate their findings into policy. In an age of slower economic growth, improvements in living standards may depend more on the skills of family planners than on those of economic planners.

WHAT'S HAPPENING AROUND THE WORLD

A poster advises Indian couples to limit the number of their children to two. India was the earliest developing nation to urge its citizens to limit family size, although the effort was neither as comprehensive as China's nor as sustained. Under the late Prime Minister Indira Gandhi, critics say, many people were pressured to undergo sterilization without understanding what it was.

Hong Kong, a 409-square-mile British colony tucked into China's southeast coast, struggles with a ballooning population. Only 57 percent of Hong Kong's people were born there. Nearly 4 million immigrants from China and elsewhere in Asia have arrived since 1947. Today, 5.3 million people live there, in an area one tenth the size of the state of Kentucky. Although the colony has a bustling economy, many of its poorest residents cannot afford adequate housing. Thousands of families make their homes on boats such as these in Hong Kong harbor.

One-child families are the ideal today in the People's Republic of China. With a population of more than 1 billion, China's leaders feared for the nation's ability to feed itself. Reminders to limit family size are constant. Sterilization is reportedly compulsory for one parent in a two-child family. Neighborhood groups police the size of local families, keeping records even on birth control practices.

Comprehension

1. Why does the economic situation in the Third World countries seem to have become worse recently?

2. According to Brown, what are the two population-control choices for Third World governments?

3. What evidence do you find in the reading that illustrates the choices referred to in question 2?

4. In paragraph 4, Brown predicts four trends for the 1980s. On the basis of current conditions, how good were his predictions?

5. Why did China develop its population policy? What is its policy?

6. What seems to have been the problem in the Indian program?

Discussion

1. What is the population policy in your country (or in a country that you know)?

2. In many countries there is a difference in attitude toward population control between the more and the less educated people. Why is that? What different attitudes and values might these groups have?

Language Practice

Fill in the blanks in the paragraph below with words from this list:

condemn	project	shrink	undergo
curb	re-examine	struggling	yield
press	rethink		

As Spain and Portugal join the Common Market community, the community will _____ a major change and the other members may have to _____ their economic policies. Economists _____ that the number of farm workers in the community will increase by 40 percent. Because of this, many farmers in France and Italy _____ the addition of Spain and Portugal to the community; these farmers are already _____ to survive. They fear that cheap fruit and vegetables from Spain and Portugal will

_____ their market. They are ready to _____ for limits to what

the Spaniards and Portuguese can sell; they want to _____ imports.

Fill in the blanks in the paragraph below with words from this list:

shift	decline	standards
deterioration	struggle	initiative
prospect	alternative	margin

Many large cities today are increasing in size because of a _____ in

population from the country to the city. This rapid increase has caused a

_____ in housing and transportation; there has been a _____ in

living _____ . As a result, living in the big cities has become a

_____ . The _____ of improvement in big city life does not

seem encouraging. One _____ would be to limit city growth, but that

decision would require the _____ of a strong, brave government.

Africa's food output was *lagging behind* its population growth. *To lag* is to
move more slowly than something or someone else. Write a sentence that describes a relationship between two institutions, two people, two developments,
and so on, using the phrase *to lag behind*. (You may use it in any verb tense.)

_____

_____

Check the meaning of the word *assumption*. On the lines below, describe an
act that depended on an assumption. For example: I assumed the hotel would
have electric outlets so I took my electric razor.

_____

_____

The Chinese often see reminders (such as the sign in the illustration) to limit their families. What do public signs in your country remind you to do? Describe one of these signs in one or two sentences.

_____

_____

_____

We all have different *ideals*. Describe your ideal for family life in two or three sentences. You might include the idea of marriage (or not), number of children, place to live, number of relatives, and so on.

_____

_____

_____

_____

_____

Choose a word from the following list and write it in the blank below next to the situation that it best describes. Be ready to explain your choices. There may be several possibilities for each situation.

harsh	bustling	massive
hard-earned	comprehensive	steady
hard-pressed	compulsory	explosive

1. _____ During the day, Michael worked in the city as a taxi-driver from about 7:00 A.M. to 5:00 P.M. To increase his income, he worked in a factory from 7:00–10:00 each evening.

2. _____ The city sidewalks were crowded with people and the streets were full of cars. Everyone seemed to be going someplace in a hurry.

3. _____ Her topic was the development of cooperative farming. She decided to begin with a study of farm remains dating from about 10,000 B.C. and continue to include twentieth century experiments.

Write a paragraph below that begins with "It's time to . . ." Complete that first sentence with a comment on some problem in your country. Write two or three sentences, stating the problem and your solution.

_____

_____

_____

_____

Use paragraph 2 of the reading as a model. In two or three sentences describe someone or some institution (a government, a school, a business, and so on) that has two choices.

_____

_____

_____

_____

Below is a description of what China did about its population problem. The ideas are not in logical order. Arrange them in a logical order by writing numbers next to the ideas; write a number 1 next to the idea that you would put first, a 2 next to the idea that you would put second, and so on.

_____ They also projected that the country couldn't support this growth.

_____ In the 1970s, Chinese leaders made a projection of the country's population growth.

_____ They decided to limit the family to one child.

_____ China was among the first countries to re-examine its population policy.

_____ The projection indicated that the population would grow 300 to 400 million more.

_____ They assumed each family would have two children.

Now write the ideas above in a logical sequence. You may combine sentences and add connecting words.

_____

_____

_____

_____

_____

_____

Follow-up Activities

1. Survey your classmates to find out how many plan to marry and have families. If they plan to marry, find out how many children they plan to have.

2. Conduct a survey (among classmates, friends, family) of attitudes toward population control. Find out how many favor control and how many do not. Ask for reasons. Find out which methods of control are preferred.

3. Choose a country and find a newspaper or magazine article that discusses one of that country's economic problems. Prepare a summary of the article.

4. Compare the food production in three countries. Find out: (1) What are the basic foods? (2) Where are the basic foods produced? (3) Does the country export foods? Which ones? (4) Does the country import foods? Which ones?

5. Look up the topic "Population" in the *Social Issues Resources Series*. Find an article related to the subject of this reading and be ready to report on it.

Topics for Further Discussion or Writing

1. What population policy do you favor? What are your reasons?

2. Is there a deterioration of cropland or forest in your country? If so, why?

3. Does your country produce most of its own food? If it imports food, what kind? How does it pay for the imports?

The Uneasy Mood of Europe's Youth

Before You Read

This article about the worries of Europe's youth appeared in *Scholastic Update*, a news magazine written for secondary school students in the United States.

Think About It

What are some common topics of conversation when you and your friends get together?

What do you think is the greatest worry among your friends in your country?

The Uneasy Mood of Europe's Youth

David Goddy

1   They dance to the sounds of Bruce Springsteen and Michael Jackson. They flock to Hollywood movies, wear bluejeans, and eat hamburgers.

2   Today's young Europeans have more in common with U.S. youth than any generation yet. But underneath the surface, they say, they're much more worried about the future than young Americans — about school and careers, about the chance of a war with the Soviet Union that would turn their homelands into a battleground. "Americans seem incredibly optimistic — naive, perhaps," says Robert Renlund, an 18-year-old exchange student from Brussels. In comparison, he sees "a wave of pessimism" among young Belgians. High school exchange students from elsewhere in Europe report much the same — a mood of uncertainty and flagging patriotism:

3   • "In Portugal," says Guida Bajanca, a 17-year-old from Lisbon, "people were very proud in the 15th century because we were the discoverers. But now nobody really cares."

4   • Satu Ahonen, a 17-year-old from Vantaa, Finland, believes others back home are "not so proud to be Finns. Not that they're ashamed, but they don't show pride."

5   • "In Italy," says Isotta Cortesi, a 17-year-old from Parma, "nobody would dream of crying over the national anthem."

6   • Young West Germans, says Christine Pressel, a 16-year-old from Hamburg, "don't feel as much for our country. In Hitler's time, they loved Germany very much. We don't want to be like that."

WORRY OVER JOBS

7 Young Europeans' number one worry, according to pollsters, is high unemployment. After 30 years of rapid growth, Europe's economic slowdown has hit young people hard. Over 40 percent of all unemployed workers in Common Market nations are under 25. That means extra pressure to do well in school and get a college degree. "Last year," recalls Renlund, "our teacher would tell us, "Try to succeed, because that will determine what job you get later."

8 The added pressure can make classes a real grind. Most European schools offer no electives or extra activities like clubs or sports, and students have little personal contact with teachers. And, in most European countries, students must pass rigid exams if they want to go on to college.

9 Even though fewer Europeans get college degrees, the ones who do aren't guaranteed a good job. For one thing, even in the best of economic times Europe's job market is hard to crack. "Portugal is a poor country, and there are not enough jobs," says Bajanca. "You see university graduates sweeping the streets." For Finns, says Ahonen, "the problem is not finding any job but getting a job that you're trained for." For another thing, European workers can't count on quick promotions. Students say that means they must make the right career choice from the beginning — a pressure that Americans, who may often change careers, don't face.

10 Few political issues have captured young Europeans' attention as the peace movement has. Last year, NATO's decision to aim new nuclear-tipped Pershing II and cruise missiles at the Soviet Union provoked massive protests around Europe. Nowhere has the peace movement been stronger or the protests larger than in West Germany, the front line in NATO's defense plans. Christine Pressel says she and her friends at home feel endangered, not protected, by the U.S. missiles and 392,000 Allied troops stationed in their nation. "There can be an accident so easily," she says.

Causes Young Europeans Say They Would Fight for

World peace	65%
Human rights	51%
Individual freedom	44%
Ending poverty	37%
Protecting environment	37%
Sexual equality	22%
National defense	18%
None	16%
Religious faith	10%
Unifying Europe	8%
Revolution	5%
No reply	3%

IMPACT OF STUDENT PROTESTS

11   Even students who come from a background of political activism say they doubt that their protests have much impact. Isotta Cortesi's mother is a member of Parma's local Communist party council. Last year, Isotta led a student strike that succeeded in winning more classrooms for her overcrowded school. Despite big student turnouts for last fall's peace marches, she feels young people cannot affect big issues, such as foreign policy. On any issue, there's the problem of being taken seriously. "My parents are completely against school strikes," Cortesi says, "because we don't get paid, so we don't lose anything."

12   Others say that a sense of uneasy resignation is perhaps the most common political attitude among young Europeans. "Everyone wants peace, right?" Guida Bajanca says with a shrug. "Everyone says that if there's a war between the U.S. and Russia, we're in the middle. If a nuclear war's going to happen, nobody can stop it. So people don't talk about it."

13   Experts say that worry about heightened U.S.-Soviet tensions is dividing social classes and raising questions about U.S. leadership. "The U.S. is in decline as a political ideal for young people," says Andy Markovitz, a professor at Boston University who is an expert on European politics. "Also, people who had vocational training and are now facing unemployment are more disillusioned than the people who went to college."

14   Pressel agrees that U.S. influence on young Germans is waning. "We used to use a lot of English words," she says. "But we don't like America that much anymore because it's scary."

15   That doesn't mean young people there are ready to give up Europe's partnership with the U.S. Even in West Germany, nearly 79 percent of people under 30 support NATO membership. Surveys also show that young Europeans distrust Soviet intentions almost as much as their parents do. Most, however, feel the West needs better relations with the Soviet bloc. "We don't love Russians," says Satu Ahonen of neutral Finland, bordering the Soviet Union, "but we have to live together."

16   Ahonen and other exchange students who talked to UPDATE have one big question about American life. "Why don't Americans dance at parties?" asks Cortesi. Adds Ahonen: "They have music but they don't dance!"

Comprehension

1.   What are some things that European and U.S. youth have in common?

2.   What do the comments by the young people from Portugal, Finland, Italy, and West Germany suggest about their attitudes toward patriotism?

3. Why is there so much pressure now for European youth to succeed in school?

4. How does the limited number of jobs affect college students when they are ready to look for a job?

5. Why has the peace movement received so much attention from young Europeans?

6. What seems to be the attitude of young Europeans toward the United States? Toward the Soviet Union?

Discussion

1. In your country, how much pressure is there for you to succeed in school? If there is pressure, what are the reasons for it?

2. What seems to be the attitude of young people in your country toward the United States and the Soviet Union?

3. What might be some ways to solve unemployment problems? What do you think of a shorter work week? What about dividing jobs so that two people have one job, each working for six months?

Language Practice

Fill in the blanks in the paragraph below with appropriate words from this list:

distrust	heightened	provoke	turnouts
doubt	issues	resignation	unemployment
give up	naive	rigid	worry about
guaranteed	pressure	slowdown	

One of the major _____ facing governments today is the high

_____ caused, in part, by a _____ in the world economy. In

some countries the lack of jobs _____ large _____ of people

who want to apply _____ to the government so that they will have

_____ jobs. In other countries, people tend to _____ ; they

_____ the ability of the government to provide jobs and they live in a

mood of _____ .

Fill in the blanks in the sentences below with appropriate words. These "mystery" words are all in the reading. The first letters of the mystery words should spell the name of a people.

1. Economic __ __ __ __ __ __ has to increase 3 percent each year to maintain the standard of living. (See paragraph 7.)

2. If we have high unemployment, students in college have __ __ __ __ __ pressure to do well in school. (See paragraph 7.)

3. A __ __ __ __ __ __ schedule is a difficult one in which there is no flexibility. (See paragraph 8.)

4. Many of the nations of Europe belong to the Common __ __ __ __ __ __. (See paragraph 7.)

5. Many people feel __ __ __ __ __ __ __ of the acts of their political leaders. (See paragraph 4.)

6. Because they are often optimistic, Americans are frequently called __ __ __ __ __. (See paragraph 2.)

7. As a result of the student __ __ __ __ __ __, the school administrators increased the number of faculty. (See paragraph 11.)

What word do the first letters of the mystery words spell?

— — — — — — —

Choose a word or phrase in the set below and use it to describe an appropriate situation in the following sentences.

EXAMPLE: in common with   European young people dance to the
                                 sounds of Bruce Springsteen and
                                 Michael Jackson. They flock to
                                 Hollywood movies.

*They have a lot in common with the young
people of the United States.*

a real grind   disillusioned   optimistic   pessimistic   pressure

1. I have classes from 9 to 12, a lab from 1 to 3, and a discussion section at 4.

   _____

   _____

   _____

2. There aren't many jobs, so students feel that they have to get a college degree to increase their chances for a job. They also feel they have to do well in college.

   _____

   _____

   _____

3. They are worried about their future. They don't think there will be enough jobs and they are afraid of nuclear weapons.

   _____

   _____

   _____

4. They think that everything will be over soon and the school will be back to normal.

   _____

   _____

   _____

5. Following vocational training school, he looked for a job, but couldn't find one.

   _____

   _____

   _____

Note the use of the *any* words with negatives:

I don't want *any* hamburgers.
We can't see *anything*.
She's not here *anymore*.

Find two sentences in the reading that use *any* in negative sentences and write them here.

1. _____

_____

2. _____

_____

Use *any* words to change each sentence below into a negative sentence.

1. The government provided jobs for the students.

_____

2. In that school, students have some personal contact with their teachers.

_____

3. They need some good music for dancing.

_____

4. They have some missiles in their country.

_____

5. There are some university graduates there who are sweeping the streets.

_____

_____

Complete this sentence:

I am (in favor/not in favor) of school strikes because _____

_____

_____

Write two sentences that describe one thing of which people in your country are proud.

_____

_____

_____

Use the first paragraph of the reading as your model. Write two or three sentences about what young people in your country do today.

_____

_____

_____

_____

Compare your secondary school to the schools described in the paragraph that begins, "The added pressure . . ." Write two or three sentences.

_____

_____

_____

Use each of the underlined words or phrases below to describe a situation with which you are familiar. Write one sentence for each.

1. We used to use a lot of English words.

_____

_____

2. European workers can't <u>count on</u> quick promotions.

   _____

   _____

3. She and her friends at home feel <u>endangered</u>, not <u>protected</u>, by the U.S. missiles.

   _____

   _____

   _____

Follow-up Activities

1. Ask a group of people what causes they would fight for. You could list some causes from the chart on p. 261 or just ask them to name their choices. Then, on the basis of the answers, prepare a chart with percentages, similar to the chart on p. 261.

2. Find out what students from different countries do at parties. When do they have parties? How long do the parties last? Where are the parties? What do people eat and drink?

3. The eighteenth century English writer Samuel Johnson wrote that "Patriotism is the last refuge of a scoundrel." Look up *refuge* and *scoundrel*. What did Johnson mean? Have the class prepare a debate on patriotism with one group defending its value and another group presenting its dangers.

4. We all borrow words from other languages. Find some words in your language that are borrowed from another language. Guess why those words were borrowed. (Very often words for food, sports, clothing, and transportation are borrowed.) Compare your list with those of other students.

_____

The Fate of the Earth

Before You Read

"The Fate of the Earth" is part of a book written by Jonathan Schell about the dangers of nuclear weapons. The book first appeared as a series of articles in *New Yorker* magazine.

Think About It

Why are nuclear weapons so dangerous?

How does the threat of nuclear destruction affect our everyday life?

The Fate of the Earth

Jonathan Schell

1   Four and a half billion years ago, the earth was formed. Perhaps a half billion years after that, life arose on the planet. For the next four billion years, life became steadily more complex, more varied, and more ingenious, until, around a million years ago, it produced mankind — the most complex and ingenious species of them all. Only six or seven thousand years ago — a period that is to the history of the earth as less than a minute is to a year — civilization emerged, enabling us to build up a human world, and to add to the marvels of evolution marvels of our own: marvels of art, of science, of social organization, of spiritual attainment. But, as we built higher and higher, the evolutionary foundation beneath our feet became more and more shaky, and now, in spite of all we have learned and achieved — or, rather, because of it — we hold this entire terrestrial creation hostage to nuclear destruction, threatening to hurl it back into the inanimate darkness from which it came. And this threat of self-destruction and planetary destruction is not something that we will pose one day in the future, if we fail to make certain precautions; it is here now, hanging over the heads of all of us at every moment. The machinery of destruction is complete, poised on a hair trigger, waiting for the "button" to be "pushed" by some misguided or deranged human being or for some faulty computer chip to send out the instruction to fire. That so much should be balanced on so fine a point — that the fruit of four and a half billion years can be undone in a careless moment — is a fact against which belief rebels. And there is another, even vaster measure of the loss, for stretching ahead from our present are more billions of years of life on earth, all of which can be filled not only with human life but with human civilization. The procession of generations that extends onward from our present leads far, far beyond the line of our sight, and, compared with these stretches of human time, which exceed the whole history of the earth up to now, our brief civilized moment is almost infinitesimal. . . . In its apparent durability, a world menaced with imminent doom is in a way deceptive. It is almost an illusion. Now we are sitting at the breakfast table drinking our coffee and reading the newspaper, but in a moment we may be inside a fireball whose temperature is tens of thousands of degrees. Now we are on our way to work, walking through the city streets, but in a moment we may be standing on an empty plain under a darkened sky looking

for the charred remnants of our children. Now we are alive, but in a moment we may be dead. Now there is human life on earth, but in a moment it may be gone.

2   Once, there was time to reflect in a more leisurely way on our predicament. In August, 1945, when the invention of the bomb was made known through its first use on a human population, the people of Hiroshima, there lay ahead an interval of decades which might have been used to fashion a world that would be safe from extinction by nuclear arms, and some voices were in fact heard counselling deep reflection on the looming peril and calling for action to head it off. On November 28, 1945, less than four months after the bombing of Hiroshima, the English philosopher Bertrand Russell rose in the House of Lords and said:

> We do not want to look at this thing simply from the point of view of the next few years; we want to look at it from the point of view of the future of mankind. The question is a simple one: Is it possible for a scientific society to continue to exist, or must such a society inevitably bring itself to destruction? It is a simple question but a very vital one. I do not think it is possible to exaggerate the gravity of the possibilities of evil that lie in the utilization of atomic energy. As I go about the streets and see St. Paul's, the British Museum, the House of Parliament, and the other monuments of our civilization, in my mind's eye I see a nightmare vision of those buildings as heaps of rubble with corpses all round them. That is a thing we have got to face, not only in our own country and cities, but throughout the civilized world.

3   Russell and others, including Albert Einstein, urged full, global disarmament, but the advice was disregarded. Instead, the world set about building the arsenals that we possess today. The period of grace we had in which to ward off the nuclear peril before it became a reality — the time between the moment of the invention of the weapons and the construction of the full-scale machinery for extinction — was squandered, and now the peril that Russell foresaw is upon us. Indeed, if we are honest with ourselves we have to admit that unless we rid ourselves of our nuclear arsenals a holocaust not only *might* occur but *will* occur — if not today, then tomorrow; if not this year, then the next. We have come to live on borrowed time: every year of continued human life on earth is a borrowed year, every day a borrowed day.

4   At present, most of us do nothing. We look away. We remain calm. We are silent. We take refuge in the hope that the holocaust won't happen, and turn back to our individual concerns. We deny the truth that is all around us. Indifferent to the future of our kind, we grow indifferent to one another. We drift apart. We grow cold. We drowse our way toward the end of the world. But if once we shook off our lethargy and fatigue and began to act, the climate would change. Just as inertia produces despair — a despair often so deep that it does not even know itself as despair — arousal and action would give us access to hope, and life would start to mend: not just life in its entirety but

daily life, every individual life. At that point, we would begin to withdraw from our role as both the victims and the perpetrators of mass murder. We would no longer be the destroyers of mankind but, rather, the gateway through which the future generations would enter the world. Then the passion and will that we need to save ourselves would flood into our lives. Then the walls of indifference, inertia, and coldness that now isolate each of us from others, and all of us from the past and future generations, would melt, like snow in spring. E. M. Forster told us, "Only connect!" Let us connect. Auden told us, "We must love one another or die." Let us love one another — in the present and across the divides of death and birth. Christ said, "I come not to judge the world but to save the world." Let us, also, not judge the world but save the world. By restoring our severed links with life, we will restore our own lives. Instead of stopping the course of time and cutting off the human future, we would make it possible for the future generations to be born. Their inestimable gift to us, passed back from the future into the present, would be the wholeness and meaning of life.

5   The task facing the species is to shape a world politics that does not rely on violence. This task falls into two parts — two aims. The first is to save the world from extinction by eliminating nuclear weapons from the earth. Just recently, on the occasion of his retirement, Admiral Hyman Rickover, who devoted a good part of his life to overseeing the development and construction of nuclear-powered, nuclear-missile-bearing submarines for the United States Navy, told a congressional committee that in his belief mankind was going to destroy itself with nuclear arms. He also said of his part in the nuclear buildup that he was "not proud" of it, and added that he would like to "sink" the ships that he had poured so much of his life into. And, indeed, what everyone is now called on to do is to sink all the ships, and also ground all the planes, and fill in all the missile silos, and dismantle all the warheads. The second aim, which alone can provide a sure foundation for the first, is to create a political means by which the world can arrive at the decisions that sovereign states previously arrived at through war. These two aims, which correspond to the aims mentioned earlier of preserving the existence of life and pursuing the various ends of life, are intimately connected. If, on the one hand, disarmament is not accompanied by a political solution, then every clash of will between nations will tempt them to pick up the instruments of violence again, and so lead the world back toward extinction. If, on the other hand, a political solution is not accompanied by complete disarmament, then the political decisions that are made will not be binding, for they will be subject to challenge by force. And if, as in our present world, there is neither a political solution nor disarmament, then the world will be held perpetually at the edge of doom, and every clash between nuclear powers will threaten to push it over the edge.

Comprehension

1. How does the author show his feelings about the terrible effects of nuclear destruction in paragraph 1?

2. Why is a "world menaced with imminent doom" deceptive?

3. What question occurred to Bertrand Russell as a result of the first atomic bomb?

4. What did Russell and Einstein suggest?

5. What two aims does the author suggest to create a world politics that doesn't rely on violence?

6. According to Schell, what attitude do most of us seem to have about the possibility of nuclear destruction? What does he say we should do?

Discussion

1. What do you think of the author's suggestions for a solution to the danger of nuclear destruction?

2. What specific actions can we take to eliminate the danger of nuclear weapons?

3. Do you ever talk about the dangers of nuclear destruction with your family? With your friends? Do the conversations end with agreement? Why or why not?

Language Practice

Substitute a word or phrase from the following list for an underlined word or phrase in the sentences below and rewrite the sentences.

indifferent to	peril	ingenious	drowse
predicament	marvels	nightmare	lethargy
fatigue	take refuge		

1. Schell feels that many of us are <u>not interested in</u> the problems created by nuclear weapons.

_____

_____

2. Sometimes the world seems so full of problems that we feel a <u>great tiredness</u> and refuse to face any of them.

     _____

     _____

3. The history of civilization is the history of <u>clever</u> human beings who created <u>wonderful examples</u> of science, art, and social organization.

     _____

     _____

4. Science discovered a great power in the release of the atom, but that discovery has put us in a <u>difficult situation</u>.

     _____

     _____

5. The <u>danger</u> of nuclear destruction increases as more countries develop their technology.

     _____

     _____

6. We <u>find protection</u> by remaining quiet and doing nothing.

     _____

7. The <u>terrible dream</u> of a nuclear holocaust has worried scientists ever since they realized the nature of nuclear power.

     _____

     _____

8. Schell claims that we do not act to eliminate nuclear weapons because we <u>stay in a condition of light sleep</u> and deny the existence of the evil around us.

    _____

    _____

Combine phrases from Column A and Column B into sentences and write them below.

A	B
The threat of destruction	send a message that would destroy us.
When the bomb was invented	we can save the world from extinction.
Unless we get rid of nuclear weapons	by which the nations of the earth can stop violence?
There are billions of years of civilization	we would act and make life possible for future generations.
By eliminating nuclear weapons	is hanging over our heads at every moment.
Is it possible to create a means	scientists advised full disarmament.
Instead of looking away	that would be lost.
A computer chip could	we can be certain of the extinction of the world.

1. _____

2. _____

3. _____

4. _____

5. _____

6. _____

7. _____

8. _____

Fill in the blanks below with appropriate words from this list:

complete	fail	precautions	solution
destroy	instruments	rebel	task
disarmament	nuclear	rely	threat
extinction	political	self-destruction	violence

There are two ways we can respond to the _____ of _____ weapons; one is _____ and the other is a _____ solution. First, for _____ disarmament, we will have to _____ the _____ of _____ that we have created. Our second _____ will be to find a political _____ so that the nations of the world will not _____ on war to arrive at their decisions. If we _____ to take these _____ , our _____ is certain.

In each set of words below there is one word that is different from the others; underline that word and be ready to tell what the other words have in common.

1. drowse   lethargy   act   fatigue

2. calm   cold   indifferent   passion

3. destroyers   perpetrators   victims

4. preserve   restore   save   destruction

5. complex   varied   simple   ingenious

6. doom   hope   nightmare   despair

7. predicament   peril   refuge   danger

Complete the following paragraph. Use ideas from paragraph 1 of the reading, but put them into your own words as much as possible.

The earth was formed _____ ago. Life developed _____ .

Then for 4 billion years, life became _____ . A million years ago

_____ and finally civilization _____ .

Paragraph 2 compares two settings. Compare what you are doing now (actions you may be doing during the week) with what you may be doing next year. Write three or four sentences.

_____

_____

_____

_____

Follow-up Activities

1. Ask a group of people this question: If your house or apartment were on fire and you could save only three things (not people), which things would you save, and why? Compare your results with those of other students.

2. The United Nations was an attempt at a political solution for problems between nations. Find out what your classmates think of the value of the UN. Ask them: Do you think the UN is an important institution? What can it do? What can't it do? If we don't have a UN, what should we have?

3. Find an article (in a contemporary newspaper or magazine) about disarmament, the UN, or nuclear weapons and be prepared to report on it to the class. You might look at the book *Hawks, Doves and Owls* by Graham T. Allison, Albert Carnesale, and Joseph Nye, Jr., which proposes some solutions to the nuclear problem.

4. Survey a group of people; ask them their choices of the three greatest human achievements in the twentieth century. Then ask them to choose the most terrible thing humans have done in this century. Compare results.

5. Find a review of Jonathan Schell's book *The Fate of the Earth* (you might look in the *New York Times*, 1982–1983) and be prepared to report on it to the class.

Chapter Review

1. What do you think should be the minimum standard of living for all human beings? What should everybody have? Remember to consider the world's limited natural resources.

2. Economic conditions are a major cause of many contemporary political problems. Did you have courses in secondary school in which economic conditions were analyzed? What subjects were discussed?

3. Compare the comments by Schell on people's attitudes toward nuclear war with those of the students who were quoted in Goddy's article.

4. Which selection in this chapter was the easiest (or hardest) to read? Why?

5. If you could change one thing about your present life, what would you change?

Credits continued from p. ii.
in a Name?" and "Can You Change Your Name?" Reprinted with permission from *Looking at the Law* by Neil L. Chayet (The Rutledge Press, 1981). **Arthur Miller,** "The Right to Die." From *Miller's Court* by Arthur Miller. Copyright © 1982 by Arthur R. Miller. Reprinted by permission of Houghton Mifflin Company. **Karen Lehrman,** "New Findings on Longer Life." From Karen Lehrman, "New Findings on Longer Life," *Consumer's Research*, February 1985. Reprinted with permission from *Consumer's Research* Magazine. **Tom Ferguson,** "Pets." From *Medical Self-Care*, Winter 1984. Reprinted by permission from *Medical Self-Care* Magazine, Pt. Reyes, CA 94956. One year subscription (6 issues) $15.00. Classified ad for pets from the *Wellesley Townsman*, June 17, 1985. Reprinted by permission. **Joseph Vitale and Robert Ross,** "A Guide to Better Health." From Joseph Vitale and Robert Ross, "A Guide to Better Health," *Bostonia*, Vol. 58, Nos. 1 and 2, January 1984. Reprinted by permission. **Anne C. Highland,** "Update on Successes of Biofeedback." From *Vogue*, February 1983. Copyright © 1983 by The Condé Nast Publications Inc. Reprinted courtesy *Vogue* and with permission of the author. **Gordon Mott,** "City of Stress." Copyright 1983 by Knight-Ridder Newspapers. Reprinted by permission. **John Hansen Mitchell,** "Five-Dog Night." From *Sanctuary*, December 1983. Reprinted by permission. **J. Bronowski,** "The Bakhtairi." Adapted from J. Bronowski, *The Ascent of Man*. Copyright © 1973 by J. Bronowski. Reprinted by permission of Little, Brown and Company, the British Broadcasting Corporation, and Angus & Robertson Publishers. **Claire Safran,** "America's Newest Immigrants." From *Redbook*, May 1980. Reprinted by permission of *Redbook* Magazine. Copyright © 1980 by The Hearst Corporation. All rights reserved. **Susan Allen Toth,** "Best Friends." Adapted from Susan Allen Toth, *Blooming: A Small-Town Girlhood*. Copyright © 1978, 1981 by Susan Allen Toth. By permission of Little, Brown and Company and the author. **Gene Light,** "My Son, The Artist." From *The New York Times*, December 9, 1984. Copyright © 1984 by The New York Times Company. Reprinted by permission. **George Theodorson,** "Romantic Love: Asian and American." Reprinted from *Social Forces* 44 (September 1965): 17–27. "Romantic Love: Asian and American" by George Theodorson. Copyright © 1965 The University of North Carolina Press. By permission. **Andrew A. Rooney,** "Herbert Hahn." From *And More by Andy Rooney*. Copyright © 1982 Essay Productions, Inc. Reprinted with the permission of Atheneum Publishers, Inc. **Linda Matchan,** "Balancing Love and Work." From Linda Matchan, "Balancing Love and Work," *The Boston Globe*, October 8, 1980. Reprinted courtesy of The Boston Globe. **Tim Smight,** "Their Work Is Play." From "Their Work Is Play," *Ford's Insider* (1979). Reprint permission granted by 13-30 Corporation. Copyright 1979. **Daniel Yankelovich,** "The New Psychological Contracts at Work." Adapted from Daniel Yankelovich, "The New Psychological Contracts at Work," *Psychology Today*, May, 1978. Reprinted by permission of the author. **Marvin J. Cetron,** "Getting Ready for the Jobs of the Future." Excerpted from Marvin J. Cetron, "Getting Ready for the Jobs of the Future," *The Futurist*, June 1983. Reprinted by permission from *The Futurist*, published by the World Future Society, 4916 St. Elmo Ave., Bethesda, MD 20814. **Paul Dickson,** "The Life of John Smith: 1985–2070." Excerpted from *The Future File* by Paul Dickson. Copyright © 1977 by Paul Dickson. Reprinted by permission of Rawson Associates and The Helen Brann Agency, Inc. **Lee Dembart,** "Why the Long Wait? — Elevator Relativity." From the *Los Angeles Times*, February 28, 1982. Copyright, 1982, Los Angeles Times. Reprinted by permission. **Penny Ward Moser,** "Getting Over Your Telephone Hangups." Excerpted from Penny Ward Moser, "Getting Over Your Telephone Hangups," *Discover*, December 1984. © Discover Magazine 1984, Time Inc. Reprinted by permission. **Diane White,** "Watches for Our Time," *The Boston Globe*, May 18, 1983. Reprinted courtesy of The Boston Globe. **Andrew A. Rooney,** "Airlines." From *And More by Andy Rooney*. Copyright © 1982 Essay Productions, Inc. Reprinted with the permission of Atheneum Publishers, Inc. "Seven Signs of Change." From *Scholastic Update*. © Graphic Chart & Map 1986. Reprinted by permission. **Lester Brown,** "It's Time to Rethink Population Policies." From *Scholastic Update*, Vol. 117, No. 8, December 14, 1984. Reprinted by permission of Scholastic Inc. **David Goddy,** "The Uneasy Mood of Europe's Youth." From *Scholastic Update*, Vol. 117, No. 6, November 16, 1984. Reprinted by permission of Scholastic Inc. **Jonathan Schell,** "The Fate of the Earth." Excerpted from *The Fate of the Earth* by Jonathan Schell. Copyright © 1982 by Jonathan Schell. Reprinted by permission of Alfred A. Knopf, Inc. and Jonathan Cape Ltd. Chart entitled "Persons in Households." From Bryant Robey and Cheryl Russell, "How America Is Changing," *American Demographics*, July/August 1982. Reprinted by permission.